I Want My Country Back!

I Want My Country Back!

We Must Stand United Again

Jon Colson

Sterling Press

Copyright © 2013 by Jon Colson

All rights reserved. No portion of this book may be reproduced, stored in a retrieval system, or transmitted in any form or by any means – electronic, mechanical, photocopy, recording, scanning, or other – except for brief quotations in critical reviews or articles without prior written permission of the publisher.

Published in Meridian, Idaho, by Sterling Press

This title may be purchased in bulk for education, business, fund-raising, or sales promotional use. For information, please email Sterling@YourVN.net

I Want My Country Back: We Must Stand United Again / Jon Colson

ISBN-13: 978-0-9894226-0-4 (Paperback)
ISBN-10: 0989422607

Printed in the United States of America

10 9 8 7 6 5 4 3 2 1

To my fellow American patriots,
who I am confident will stand together and prove to the world once again that the American spirit is alive and well and will defend liberty.

The proverbial frog is about to leave the pot.

Contents

Introduction..9

Chapter 1: The US Constitution:
                An Overview.......................................13

Chapter 2: The Intent of The Founders 21

Chapter 3: How Did We Get So Far Off Track............29
- From the Beginning.....................................31
- The 17th Amendment:
  The Final Nail in the Coffin.......................... 37
- Judicial Abuses..39
- Executive Abuses...51
- Legislative Abuses..61
- Sooooo,..67
- How Far Have We Gone?..............................73

Chapter 4: United Again...................................... 85
- How Do We Get it Back? 87
- Wrapping it All Up....................................93
- A Final Thought..95

Appendix 1: The Constitution of the United
                  The United States of America..................97

Appendix 2: The Kentucky Resolutions of 1798.......139

Appendix 3: Why Congress Never Changes............151

About the Author...155

Introduction

Are you happy with your state and federal government? If you answered no, you're reading the right book. If you answered yes, you are happy with the government, then go back to sleep and let the rest of us handle this mess.

If you are not angry with the current state of our government, you're not paying attention. This is an absolute truth. I don't care whether you are Democrat, Republican, Independent, Libertarian, or whatever; our government is a mess on every level. Furthermore; we have never been so polarized. We do not seem able to agree on anything that our government is doing. We have become polar opposites on so many issues that it seems we are two different species. But think again. I personally believe that we *can* agree on at least some fundamentals. Is there anyone who does not want a strong economy, a land of opportunity, freedom, solid wages, and reliable jobs? No. We might define things differently and have opposing views on how to get there, but I believe that the polarization is intentionally caused by a government that wants to keep us arguing so that we do not pay attention to what they are doing.

If you are like most people, you have either given up or are beating your head against the wall trying to figure out what you can do about it. The idea that, "You can't fight City Hall" has led to, "You can't fight the government at any level."

Well, my friends, here is the problem with those statements. We ARE City Hall. We ARE the state and federal governments.

Do not worry if you have forgotten those facts. The politicians who sit in those seats have forgotten them, too. It is time for us to remember that ours is a government of the people, by the people and for the people. When we remember that, it is time to re-implement that philosophy by reminding those who are supposed to represent us in those bodies of government. Notice that I did not and never will refer to those representing us as "political leaders." We do not elect them to lead, we elect them to represent. This is a huge distinction that all of us must understand and embrace once again.

This book is a look at four political realities. It is written so that anyone at any level can easily understand. However, it is written from a depth of study that few ever take the time to reach. In it, we will observe:

- The fundamentals of the Constitution - what they are and what they mean.
- What has happened that has allowed us to stray so far from those fundamentals?
- Where we are today?
- How can we get back to the Constitution?

You may be asking yourself, "Who is Jon Colson and why is he writing this book?"

My answer is simple. I am one who has a passion for America and everything that she stands for. I am a man who has spent thousands of hours studying the Constitution, the founding documents, the journals of the founders, the state ratification documents, and writings of the founders in the years following.

I am a Christian who believes that God has blessed this nation for almost 200 years but no longer, because we have pushed Him out. I will not get preachy here. I will only say that if you pray, now is a good time. If you do not pray, it is a good time to start.

Finally, I am a husband, father, and grandfather. I want to leave a country for my grandchildren that is better than it was when I entered it. The path that we are on will not lead us to that conclusion. However, as long as there is breath in me, I will continue to fight for this great nation in any way that I am capable.

This book is one battle in that fight. I hope you will join me…

Chapter 1

The US Constitution: An Overview

First, is the US Constitution flawless? No. It has its problems. Examples include the fact that it allowed for slavery, and it assumed that women were second class citizens. The founders themselves had no illusions of perfection either, so they allowed for amendments which were designed to, and have since fixed, those and other problems.

On the other hand, the US Constitution was a brilliantly conceived document compiled by a group of very intelligent men. A brief summary of our US Constitution* follows. A complete copy can be found in Appendix 1.

*Note: any direct copying of the Constitution or any other founding document is strictly with original spelling and punctuation. Any underlining is mine and used for emphasis.

~~~~~~

The US Constitution includes several parts. Each has its own purpose and meaning. They are:

- **_Preamble_**: An overview of the body of the original Constitution. The preamble holds no legal status within the Constitution. It is simply a statement of the purpose of the document that follows it. We can gain an understanding of the intent of the founders from the statement the Preamble makes.

- **_The Constitution_**: This is the body of the original document. It is broken down into Articles, Sections, and Paragraphs. Each article has a very distinct purpose within the document. The sections and paragraphs are defining characteristics of the article that they fall under. Picture the layout of a traditional outline. The Articles are as follows:

  - **Article One**:
    Defines Congress as the Legislative branch of the government.

Establishes that laws are created here; sets very specific limitations on the power of Congress.

Sets forth specific prohibitions of state authority.

➢ **Article Two**:
Defines the office of the President and the rest of the Executive branch of the government.

Sets forth the qualifications, election protocol.

Defines the very limited authority of the President.

➢ **Article Three**:
Defines the federal court system, appointments, hierarchy of the Supreme Court and other federal courts.

Defines very specific instances where the Supreme Court is the highest authority. This is also a finite list defining very limited powers.

➢ **Article Four**:
Defines the process by which new states can be admitted,

Declares that a citizen of *any state* is a citizen of the United States.

Establishes the manner in which one state's laws impact citizens when they cross state lines.

➤ **Article Five**:
Puts very specific requirements as to how the Constitution can be amended and lays out the process for how that is to be done.

➤ **Article Six**:
Accepts the debts of the nation that were incurred prior to the adoption of the Constitution

Defines the US Constitution as highest law of the land, followed by laws and treaties passed according to constitutional methods and limits.

➤ **Article Seven:**
Defines the requirements for ratification of the Constitution and clearly spells out that it was unanimously ratified by all 13 states.

- ***Preamble to the Bill of Rights***: Like the first preamble, this is simply a declaration of intent. It spells out why the Bill of Rights was added and what the founders intended these first ten amendments to accomplish.

- ***The Bill of Rights***: This is a collection of the first ten amendments to the US Constitution. They were added because several states demanded it before they would ratify the original document. They called for more protections from abuse of power by the federal government. Rather than rewrite the entire document, they made the changes that were demanded in ten separate and distinct amendments.

Here is a very short version:
- **Amendment I** – Freedom of speech, religion, and assembly.

- **Amendment II** – Right to keep and bear arms.

- **Amendment III** – Citizens not required to house soldiers.

- **Amendment IV** – Right to privacy.

- **Amendment V** – No requirement of self-incrimination; cannot be charged with the same crime twice, and cannot be deprived of life, liberty, or property without due process of law.

- **Amendment VI** – Right to a fair and speedy trial.

- **Amendment VII** – Right to a trial by jury.

- **Amendment VIII** – Prohibits excessive bail.

- **Amendment IX** – State powers listed are not all-inclusive.

➢ **Amendment X** – Federal powers listed here ARE all-inclusive.

- *<u>Amendments 11-27</u>* - The remaining Amendments have been passed individually, over the years, rather than as a group. This process was provided as the only way to amend the Constitution and was done as early as 1795 and as late as 1992. A very short version of each follows:

➢ **Amendment XI** – The power of the federal court was limited even more, removing their jurisdiction in a lawsuit against one state by a citizen of another state or a subject of a foreign power.

➢ **Amendment XII** – Very specifically amends and defines how the president is elected.
➢ **Amendment XIII** – Abolishes slavery.

➢ **Amendment XIV** – Establishes that anyone born in the US is US Citizen; defines voters as citizens age 21 or above; prohibits anyone who has been hostile against the government from being elected; guarantees that the bills incurred by the United States will always be paid.

➢ **Amendment XV** – Establishes that the right to vote will not be denied to any race or former slave.

- **Amendment XVI** – Determines that Congress has the authority to tax income.

- **Amendment XVII** – Senators shall be elected by the people instead of by the state legislatures.

- **Amendment XVIII** – Alcohol is prohibited.

- **Amendment XIX** – Recognized a woman's right to vote.

- **Amendment XX** – A president's term will start Jan 20; Congress's terms will start Jan 3. Congress must meet at least once per year. If the president-elect dies between election and the start of term, the vice-president becomes president and appoints a vice-president.

- **Amendment XXI** – Repeals alcohol prohibition.

- **Amendment XXII** – Establishes that a president cannot be elected for more than two terms.

- **Amendment XXIII** – Determines that the seat of the federal government, (currently the District of Columbia), shall have representation in presidential elections in the form of electors.

- **Amendment XXIV** – Prohibits any poll tax or financial cost for voting.

➤ **Amendment XXV** – Establishes succession in the event the president dies or is otherwise unable to perform duties.

➤ **Amendment XXVI** – Lowers voting age to 18.

➤ **Amendment XXVII** – If Congress votes for raises in salaries, said raises will not take effect until after the start of a Congressman's next term.

There you have it. The US Constitution, both preambles, the Bill of Rights, and Amendments 11-27 combined total just over 8,000 words. In that short space, our founding fathers laid out the fundamentals of our entire federal government.

Chapter 2

The Intent of the Founders

The "intent" of the founders of our country has been the subject of many debates. Some say that it is a living document that changes with the times; others say that it is to be followed exactly as written. Some claim that it grants the federal government the power to expand and change as necessary, while others say that it sets strict limits. How can we possibly know who is right? There is nobody to ask, right? Actually, believe it or not, we can ask the founders.

First, was the Constitution written to be interpreted with the times? Are we to change the way we read the Constitution because of the date? Times change. Should the government not change along with those times? That would be considered progress, right?

On the other side of that argument, some people say that it was written as strict rules to be followed. How can the Constitution hold any weight if it can be changed on a whim based on something as simple as the date?

Who is right? We need input from the people who wrote the Constitution; the founders who spelled it out.

Article V of the Constitution sets forth the amendment process. It dictates exactly what is required in order to make changes to the Constitution. Here is the first part of Article V:

> *"The Congress, whenever two-thirds of both Houses shall deem it necessary, shall propose Amendments to this Constitution, or, on the Application of the Legislatures of two-thirds of the several States, shall call a Convention for proposing Amendments..."*

The rest of Article V talks about how the amendment shall be ratified. I'm not sure how it can be spelled out any more clearly; <u>The way to change the Constitution is through the amendment process.</u>

Nowhere else in the Constitution does it say or imply that the Constitution can be changed, be that because of the date, various interpretations or the whim of a rogue court, legislation or president.

Article V is also clear as to who can propose amendments. A point to keep in mind is that the Supreme Court is not mentioned.

Now, to answer the question as to whether the Constitution was written with the understanding that it will change with the times, the founders proclaimed a resounding "yes." However, they also spelled out exactly how these changes must be accomplished. They not only made it difficult to do so, but they spelled out a process requiring approval by the states. The federal government has no power to add to or change their authority without the approval of three-quarters of the state legislatures. Any changes without this process would clearly be prohibited. If the Constitution had been written to change with the times automatically by "interpretation", then Article V would not have been necessary.

The second major argument as to the founders' intent is whether or not the federal government has the authority to expand as needed. Some would say that as the needs of the nation expand, so will the federal government naturally. Others say that the Constitution established very strict limits on the federal government, and that any expansion is unconstitutional.

Back to the founders. They put forth a Constitution that specifically defined the federal government. How did the states respond? Let's look at the second preamble for this.

Many of you may be thinking, "What do you mean the 'second preamble'? The public school that I attended did not teach anything about a second preamble."

It's okay; neither did mine. I was so conditioned to what was taught in school that I studied the Constitution for over a year, but actually skipped it the whole time. When I discovered it, I was shocked to see how much light it shed on this argument.

The second preamble is the Preamble to the Bill of Rights. The first clause spells out exactly why the Bill of Rights was written. Here is that clause:

> **"THE** *Conventions of a number of the States, having at the time of their adopting the Constitution, expressed a desire, <u>in order to prevent misconstruction or abuse of its powers, that further declaratory and restrictive clauses should be added</u>: And as extending the ground of public confidence in the Government, <u>will best ensure the beneficent ends of its institution</u>.*"

Several states were concerned about the term "misconstruction or abuse of powers." Misconstruction means that the federal government could interpret the Constitution in ways that might enable them to abuse their powers. What did the states do about it? They created a Bill of Rights that specifically spelled out some specific rights that the federal government acknowledged and could not infringe upon. They went further than that with the 9th and 10th Amendments.

These were written to declare once again the limits on the federal government. Although the powers were specifically enumerated, the individual states wanted to again declare the "beneficent ends," or limits of the federal government. Here are the 9th and 10th Amendments:

> **Amendment IX**
> *"The enumeration in the Constitution, of certain rights, shall not be construed to deny or disparage others retained by the people."*

> **Amendment X**
> *"The powers not delegated to the United States by the Constitution, nor prohibited by it to the States, are reserved to the States respectively, or to the people."*

The 9th Amendment was written so that the federal government could not declare that the rights in Amendments 1-8 were the only rights of the people. Quite the opposite of the clause that follows.

The 10th Amendment is the amendment that the federal government seems to love to ignore the most. The limited powers of each branch of the federal government are clearly spelled out and defined. The 10th amendment goes a step further and declares that the *enumeration of powers* shall be construed as a *limit of powers* of the federal government. If it is a power that is not specifically granted to the federal government or prohibited to the states within the Constitution, then it is a power that resides with the states or the people.

Unlike the 9th, the founders declared that any defined powers are the limits of the federal government.

Without completely ignoring the 9th and 10th Amendments, one cannot logically say that the federal government has the authority to expand itself. Even if two-thirds of both houses of Congress decide it necessary to propose amendments to the Constitution, they cannot do so without the approval of three-quarters of the states.

Another clause often cited as giving power to the president to expand the government through appointment, is Article II, Section 2, Paragraph 2. Here it is in its entirety:

> *"He shall have Power, <u>by and with the Advice and Consent of the Senate</u>, to make Treaties, <u>provided two thirds of the Senators present concur;</u> and he shall nominate, and by <u>and with the Advice and Consent of the Senate,</u> shall appoint Ambassadors, other public Ministers and Consuls, Judges of the supreme Court, and all other Officers of the United States, whose Appointments are not herein otherwise provided for, and <u>which shall be established by Law:</u> but the Congress may by Law vest the Appointment of such inferior Officers, as they think proper, in the President alone, in the Courts of Law, or in the Heads of Departments."*

The first thing to be pointed out here is that almost anything that the president does in terms of appointment requires either Senate approval or a power relinquished to him by Congress without approval. There are two words here that those who claim expansion powers are given to the president like to ignore, and those are "by law." This means that the president can appoint to positions which were created by writing a law to create those positions. "By law" means that the position itself must be created by the legislature, *not by the president*. It also means that such a role must be created within the limited powers of Congress. In other words, if it is required to fulfill the limited federal role, and Congress creates the position, then the president can appoint a person to fill that position. Whether he is required to get senate approval is determined by Congress.

To clarify, only Congress can create a position, agency, or department of government and it has to be within the very limited powers of the federal government. Then and only then can the president appoint someone to such a position or department and, unless the approval power of the Senate is relinquished, the appointment still needs approval.
Once again, nowhere is it stated that any entity has the authority to expand power outside of the amendment process. That requires the permission of the states.

If the federal government is clearly limited in size and scope; if it does not have the power to expand itself without approval of the states, and if it does not adjust with time… how did it get so big and how did it gain so much power? In a word… unconstitutionally.

Chapter 3

How Did We Get So Far Off Track?

Unfortunately, no level of protection has ever stopped people from trying to breach security. It doesn't matter whether it's castle walls, home security systems, security guards in businesses, or even contracts. There will always be those who try to break through protection. In the case of the US Constitution, we are talking about a contract.

This particular contract was designed to define the government and the very strict limits placed on that government. No matter how many ways the framers declared limitations on the power of the federal government, those limitations have not stopped legislators, judges, presidents and even leaders of unconstitutional agencies from seizing powers that they do not have.

No matter how much protection one has, someone will try to breach it. In this case, the people who are attempting to breach that protection are not unlike thieves trying to break into a secured property. They are like snakes; constrictors trying to squeeze the life out of the people.

From the Beginning:

From the very beginnings of this nation, our federal government has been trying to expand its own power. It was happening so frequently that in just over a decade after the Constitution was signed, Thomas Jefferson, realizing the threat to our nation, wrote the Kentucky Resolution of 1798. Some claim that the author of this resolution is unknown, however when you compare it to Jefferson's other writings, it is very clearly his work.

You can read the Kentucky Resolution in its entirety in Appendix 2. The sections pertinent to this book are one, seven, and eight. One and seven will be cited in entirety here. Section Eight is very lengthy, so I have copied only those parts that are necessary for this discussion. These citations will be exactly as written with the exception that any underlining is my own.

> **Section 1**: *Resolved, That the several States composing the United States of America, are not united on the principle of unlimited submission to their general government; but that, by a compact under the style and title of a Constitution for the United States, and of amendments thereto, <u>they constituted a general government for special purposes — delegated to that government certain definite powers, reserving, each State to itself, the residuary mass of right to their own self-government; and that</u>*

whensoever the general government assumes undelegated powers, its acts are unauthoritative, void, and of no force: that to this compact each State acceded as a State, and is an integral part, its co-States forming, as to itself, the other party: *that the government created by this compact was not made the exclusive or final judge of the extent of the powers delegated to itself; since that would have made its discretion, and not the Constitution, the measure of its powers;* but that, as in all other cases of compact among powers having no common judge, each party has an equal right to judge for itself, as well of infractions as of the mode and measure of redress."

In Section One, Jefferson points out that the federal government is limited and the bulk of the rights remain with the states. He clarifies that any assumption of undelegated powers are void and have no power. This will later be agreed to by the US Supreme Court in *Marbury v. Madison; 1803*. Furthermore, Jefferson clarifies that the federal government is not the final authority in determining what powers were delegated. It is clear and obvious, as Jefferson pointed out, that if the federal government were to determine what powers were given to it, then it would be by self-discretion, not by the Constitution, that its powers would be measured.

The very idea that the states agreed to delegate limited powers to a central government, yet gave that central government the authority to determine what those powers entailed is absurd.

For example. Let's say that you gave me the authority to fish in a creek that runs through your back yard. We drew up a contract that allowed me an easement to walk down the bank to a certain point and fish. I later decide that a day fishing trip is not long enough; I need to be able to set up camp. After a few nights I realize that my campsite is not very comfortable, so I build a small shack. I then realize that your home would be more comfortable than my shack. After reviewing the contract, I decide that, by allowing me to fish on your property, you are thereby allowing me the right to fish indefinitely. Furthermore, that must mean that I can live in your home, drive your cars, wear your clothes and eat your food.

At this point, you stress that it is your land and your rules. I do not like that, and I tell you that you cannot add any rules that violate mine. I tell you that I will be the one to determine whether your rules violate mine or not. This is EXACTLY what our federal government has done.

> **Section 7:** *"Resolved, <u>That the construction applied by the General Government </u>(as is evidenced by sundry of their proceedings) to those parts of the Constitution of the United States which delegate to Congress a power "to lay and collect taxes, duties, imports, and excises, to pay the debts, and provide for*

the common defense <u>and general welfare of the United States</u>," and "to make all laws which shall be <u>necessary and proper</u> for carrying into execution the powers vested by the Constitution in the government of the United States, or in any department or officer thereof, <u>goes to the destruction of all limits prescribed to their powers by the Constitution: that words meant by the instrument to be subsidiary only to the execution of limited powers, ought not to be so construed as themselves to give unlimited powers, nor a part to be so taken as to destroy the whole residue of that instrument:</u> that the proceedings of the General Government under color of these articles, will be a fit and necessary subject of revisal and correction, at a time of greater tranquility, while those specified in the preceding resolutions call for immediate redress."

Here Jefferson points out that powers such as taxation, and phrases such as "general welfare" and "necessary and proper" should not be used to expand the general government, but relate to those powers delegated, not powers contrived, expanded, stolen or presumed.

This is very much aligns with the whole of the Constitution and of the 9th and 10th amendments which combine to reassert that the Constitution grants very finite powers to the federal government, and all other government powers, to rest with the states and the people.

In section 8, Jefferson talked about the solution for such abuses of authority. Here is the text that is relevant:

> **Section 8** - - *"therefore this commonwealth is determined, as it doubts not its co-States are, to submit to undelegated, and consequently unlimited powers in no man, or body of men on earth: <u>that in cases of an abuse of the delegated powers, the members of the general government, being chosen by the people, a change by the people would be the constitutional remedy; but, where powers are assumed which have not been delegated, a nullification of the act is the rightful remedy: that every State has a natural right in cases not within the compact, (casus non fœderis) to nullify of their own authority all assumptions of power by others within their limits:</u> that without this right, they would be under the dominion, absolute and unlimited, of whosoever might exercise this right of judgment for them: that nevertheless, this commonwealth, from motives of regard and respect for its co States, has wished to communicate with them on the subject: that with them alone it is proper to communicate, they alone being parties to the compact, and solely authorized to judge in the last resort of the powers exercised under it, <u>Congress being not a party, but merely the creature of the compact, and subject as to its assumptions of power to the final judgment of those by whom, and for whose use itself and its powers were all created and modified.</u>"*

Here Jefferson shows that there are two types of abuses requiring two different solutions. First, if the elected officials abuse the powers that they were given, then the rightful remedy is to replace them. In other words, the people elected these officials; therefore the people can remove and replace them. The *people* have the final say.

The second type of abuse would be assumed authority. If Congress and, by extension, the federal government, assume powers that are not delegated to them, then the states have the right to nullify those laws by declaring that to do so is not within the powers granted to the federal government. Jefferson did not mention the executive or legislative branches here as they are not granted any authority to create laws.

Another important distinction is that Congress is not even a party to the compact. The states are the parties to the compact. Congress is a "creature" that was created by the compact. This distinction makes it clear that Congress and the federal government have no say whatsoever as to the limits placed upon the federal government. The federal government has no place at a negotiating table; no standing in court against the states, and no executive authority to create or interpret laws. That power rests with the states.

Amendment XVII: Another Nail in the Coffin

What was sold to the voters as a way for US citizens to gain more control of their government could only have been an intentional power grab by the federal government. The founders created two chambers of Congress. The House of Representatives was referred to as "The People's House." The Senate was designed to protect states' rights. For this reason, the legislatures of each state selected their own US Senators to represent their states. That way, Senators were beholden to the states, not to the people. The 17th Amendment changed all of that. It declared that Senators would be elected by the people of the state.
It's easy to see how the people would be quick to jump on the idea that Senators would be accountable to the people rather than the state. However, this amendment left a large hole in the government in that no longer was anyone representing the states and states' rights.

The effects of this have slowly evolved over the years, bringing us to a place where individual state governments believe that they are subject to the federal government's directives. The federal government collectively acts as if it is the master of all. The people have come to believe that there is no hope of stopping the over-reaching federal government. Yet, when four

US Senators were asked who they represent, they all said "the people of my state."

If our US Senators do not even understand their job or who they represent, is it any wonder that the responsibility of protecting states' rights is no longer being accomplished? Senators don't even know that's their job. When considered in this perspective, it also becomes clear why members of Congress believe they have no limits as to what they can do. Nobody is fighting against this abuse of power.

Judicial Abuses

Today we hear terms like "activist judges" and "legislating from the bench," and we can certainly point to actions by courts to make and change laws on every level right up to the Supreme Court of the United States, hereafter (SCOTUS). The court systems do <u>not</u> have the authority to create or alter law and, although the practice is becoming more and more common, it is absolutely unconstitutional.

Without a doubt the ongoing abuse that has endured the test of time for over 200 years, comes from the case of *Marbury v Madison 1803*. The case involved a large number of last minute appointments of judges by President Adams during the lame duck session after President Jefferson had been elected, but prior to his taking office. The significance of the case itself is of very little consequence. The significance of the ruling, however, has had enduring and damaging impact ever since.

In *Marbury v. Madison*, the winning opinion was written by Chief Justice John Marshall. Not only did the court rule as to whether or not Mr. Marbury should get the commission as a judge that he was seeking, but Chief Justice Marshall expanded the scope of the SCOTUS dramatically.

Constitutionally, the SCOTUS has original jurisdiction, (meaning cases can be brought directly to them) in some instances and appellate jurisdiction, (meaning the case must first have been heard by a lower court), in other cases. The Constitution is very clear in defining each. The powers and responsibilities of the SCOTUS are finite and defined just like the executive and legislative branches.

These are the very limited number of instances where the US Supreme Court has any judicial authority:

- All cases affecting Ambassadors, other public Ministers and Consuls outside of the US

- All cases of admiralty and maritime jurisdiction

- All controversies in which the United States shall be a Party, i.e., if the federal government is sued

- When acting as an arbiter between any number of states

- Cases between a state and citizens of another state or subjects of any foreign state (that cross state or international lines)

- Cases between citizens of different states (again crossing state lines)

- Cases involving citizens of the same state claiming lands under grants of different States

> Cases between a state or the citizens thereof, and foreign states, citizens or subjects (again crossing state lines.)

It should also be noted that the 11th Amendment eliminated the SCOTUS jurisdiction under the 5th bullet when citizens or subjects of any foreign state sue a state, limiting the jurisdiction of the SCOTUS even more.

Nowhere did it allow for the power of judicial review. It did not allow for the SCOTUS to determine the constitutionality of a state or federal law.

In *Marbury v. Madison*, Chief Justice Marshall agreed. The power of judicial review is the power to determine whether a law is in line with or in violation of the Constitution. Chief Justice Marshall went so far in his ruling as to state that the SCOTUS did not have the power of judicial review because it had been granted in the Constitution, but because ... are you ready for this .... the SCOTUS <u>should have</u> the power of judicial review.

Yes, you read that correctly. Nowhere in the US Constitution was the SCOTUS granted the authority to review laws for constitutionality. Chief Justice Marshall and five other Supreme Court justices at the time stole that power for the SCOTUS because they felt that was where that power *should* lie.

In legal circles, this is referred to as an implied power. It is wrong historically, philosophically, logically, and constitutionally. The Founders covered that in the 9th and 10th amendments and that any undefined power was clearly given to the states. No "implied" necessary.

Since that ruling, the SCOTUS and the federal government have used that ruling in overturning state and confirming federal laws. It has also been used as a way for the federal government to block the implementation of state laws by suing states and having the Supreme Court rule that the new state law violates the Constitution. This goes right back to the scenario of my right to fish on your land. The federal government is telling the body that created it what it can and cannot do in its own state without any such authority to do so.

Let's look at another comparable scenario. You and your wife have two children. Your son, Legi, (it's a family name), does not like your rule that chocolate pie is not for breakfast. Legi demands that this prohibition of pie for breakfast is not within the powers of the parents, because…he *wants* pie for breakfast. Who gets to decide whether the rule stands? His sister, Judi, of course.

The only way to make this comparison more accurate would be to say that Judi's belly wanted pie for breakfast and her mouth made the ruling. The parents (states) created Judi (the federal government) and one part of Judi wants to be the judge between another part of her and the parents.

Yes, that sounds silly. It is silly. It is absurd to think that a body created will dictate rules to the people who created the body and established the rules to begin with. Yet, that is exactly what the federal government has created in our system of government. The states created the federal government. Now the federal government rules the states and determines what powers the states have.

Furthermore, if a branch of the federal government gets into a battle with one or more states... another branch of the federal government makes the decision. Ridiculous? Absolutely.

This all stems from Chief Justice Marshall's ruling in *Marbury v Madison in 1803* that the SCOTUS has that power because they *should*.

There is another major flaw in that ruling. The majority opinion stated that the Constitution did not spell out where the power of judicial review would lie. This was incorrect. Early in my studies, I believed this to be true. I based my entire premise that the states had final authority on the same idea as Jefferson had in the Kentucky Resolution. I simply believed that the federal government was a product of the document and not a party to it, so the states would have final say. While this is true, it is only one of the reasons why it is clear that the states are the final arbiters of whether a law is constitutional and of the limits of power vested in the federal government.

Another reason that the states are the final arbiters is spelled out in the scenarios above. It is absurd to think that, in the absence of something being spelled out, it is a given that the creation would therefore have more authority than the creator. This scenario can happen, such as with executive boards, but it is always clearly and legally spelled out. In the Constitution, the opposite is also clearly and legally spelled out.

Further study has led me to the clearest answer of them all. The US Constitution spells out exactly who the final arbiters are. Here is how:

- First, the Constitution clearly spells out the powers of each branch of government. All authority that they have is defined and finite.

- Second, it spells out the things that the states cannot do. There are powers that the state does not have, and they are defined as specifically as the limits of the federal government.

- Finally, the Tenth Amendment is the key: "The powers not delegated to the United States by the Constitution, nor prohibited by it to the States, are reserved to the States respectively, or to the people."

The power of judicial review was not granted to the federal government. Even Chief Justice Marshall admitted that. It was also not prohibited by the states. This is exactly in line with Jefferson's statements in the Kentucky Resolution. If they are abusing powers that were granted to them, then the people, (voters) have the authority. If they are trying to expand their power, it is the states that have the power of nullification. I would add that it is not only within the authority of the states, but also the duty of the state legislators because they have sworn to uphold and defend the Constitution.

Ironically, in *Marbury v. Madison*, it was also ruled that any law which violates the Constitution is null and of no effect. They got this one right, however, the decision as to which laws violate the Constitution lies with the states.

The common abuses by the US Supreme Court and other federal courts are in their "finding rights" in the Constitution that do not exist. One of the most well-known examples of this is Roe v. Wade. In this landmark case, the Supreme Court declared that a woman has the Constitutional right to have an abortion.

We can put the "it is a woman's body" argument aside. We can put the "it is murder" argument aside. We can put every argument for or against whether abortion should be legal aside. What cannot be ignored in this discussion is the fact that abortion is NOT a Constitutional right. The federal government has no jurisdiction here either.

Whether you are for abortion or against it, the fact is that the power to determine whether abortion is legal does not rest with the federal government. According to the Constitution, that decision rests with the states. There is nothing in the Constitution that would allow a woman to have an abortion. Furthermore, there is nothing in the Constitution that would allow the federal government, including the judicial branch, the power to rule on it.
Absurd is the fact that the ruling is based on the 14th Amendment and the Due Process Clause (DPC).

"Nor shall any State deprive any person of life, liberty, or property, without due process of law;"

Seven of the Supreme Court justices determined that part of liberty is privacy, and that a woman's right to privacy gives her the right to an abortion. If a woman can do what she wants in private, why can't she murder her husband? How about a politician, as long as it is in private?

Some claim that because it is her body she can do what she wants and it is a private matter. Others point out that she is not killing her own body, but that of a life inside of her.

The argument that abortion is a privacy issue falls flat. This is an argument about when a human life becomes a human life. Unless that matter is defined by an amendment to the US Constitution, then that definition rests with the states, according to the Constitution. In any case, the SCOTUS has no say in the matter. Ironically, if the 14th Amendment protects life, liberty, and property, how can it be construed to grant the right to *take* life? It is more logical to view it as protecting all human life, born and unborn. The argument for the 14th being *against* abortion is stronger than it is for guaranteeing some hidden right to abortion.

Whether you think that a woman should have the right to get an abortion or not, it takes stretching, bending, twisting and *interpreting,* the Constitution to make that explanation fit. And it takes breaking the Constitution to pretend that the US Supreme Court has any say in the matter.

Another abuse by the courts came recently in the battle over gay marriage. Again, this has nothing to do with which side one is on. Many of my Christian friends do not like these facts, but the SCOTUS was mostly right on this one. The Defense of Marriage Act (DOMA) was passed and signed into law by Bill Clinton. Last month, the SCOTUS ruled DOMA unconstitutional. They were right. The federal government has no business defining or ruling on marriage. However…

- ➢ Even though the Congress had no business getting involved, it was equally wrong for the SCOTUS to even hear the case. Any statement that gay marriage is unconstitutional should come from the states.

➢ The SCOTUS ruled that the federal government has no authority in the matter. However, if they had the authority to hear and rule on the case, they should have also legally clarified that neither the courts, nor the federal government has the authority to overturn the will of the people in a state matter.

➢ This would have included the California State Supreme Court, which also has no authority in the matter. Instead, the SCOTUS ruling turned over a federal court ruling which had overturned the California Supreme Court ruling.

➢ It should also be pointed out that, until the law is nullified by the states, the president of the United States does not have the right to pick and choose which laws are enforced. It is dereliction of duty for President Obama to decide that the law should not be followed.

All this may sound confusing, but what it boils down to is that the SCOTUS removed all federal courts from ruling, but not the state court. Therefore, by default, the California Supreme Court's ruling stands. That ruling overturned the will of the people, but lacked the legal right to do so. All in all, the SCOTUS should not have ruled, but did…mostly right, but that ruling led to a wrong conclusion.

Far and away, the two most common abuses by the judicial branch are the number of state laws which have been wrongly overturned, and even more unconstitutional - federal laws upheld.

Executive Abuses

The term "Executive Order," is a term that appears nowhere in the US Constitution. It takes an amazing amount of spinning and vocabulary contortionist acts to even pretend that such power rests within the executive branch of the federal government. I have looked and researched and dug and surfed for any substantial basis for the president having such authority. It does not exist.

The president's basic powers are limited to appointing his cabinet, judges and other offices which have been created by law; and to be commander in chief of the military. Even these powers are limited because Congress is the only body that can declare war, which means a president cannot take us to war without congressional approval.-- Well, according to the Constitution anyway.-- Also, the Senate must approve any appointments made by the president, thereby further controlling the president's authority in that area.

I think it is important to note that the power to appoint is specifically limited by the Constitution to those whose offices are created "by law." There is only one reason that this would have been put there. It was yet another limiting phrase added so that the president cannot create agencies or other bodies. The phrase "by law" indicates that any such agency must be created by

Congress and by extension must be within the limited powers of Congress.

Some big government fans like to claim that the power to appoint grants power to create any agency and appoint any office that the president sees fit. This is obviously not the case. We see throughout the Constitution very strict limitations on power. A blanket authorization such as this is in no way substantiated, logical, or fitting in a document designed to restrict power. Add the fact that all powers of the president have to be approved by Congress; a blanket power such as this is absurd.

What kinds of laws have been created through executive orders? How long have they been around? The answers might shock you. Executive orders have been used almost as long as the United States has existed as a nation. Franklin D. Roosevelt remains as the king of the executive order. He issued 3,522 executive orders while president. To date, there have been almost 14,000 executive orders from Presidents Lincoln through Obama. Executive orders were not numbered until early in the 20th Century, but the state department went back to the presidency of Abraham Lincoln and started numbering at #1.

Some presidents have abused this unconstitutional authority a little and others have abused it a lot. Executive orders are being used more and more aggressively lately and they are becoming a favorite way for presidents to get what they want when Congress will not do their bidding.

In 1998, a presidential aide to Bill Clinton, Paul Begala, put the controversy into perspective.

"Stroke of the pen. Law of the land. Kinda cool," he said, boasting how the Clinton machine was able to simply dictate whatever it wanted.

More recently, President George W. Bush signed a few very controversial executive orders:
- 13233 expanded the government's wiretap surveillance authority to include warrantless taps inside the United States as long as the other end of the line was a known terrorist outside of the US.

- 13440 allowed the federal government to detain enemies caught on the battlefield fighting against our military to be detained indefinitely without trial in Guantanamo Bay, Cuba.

- 13279 declared that faith-based organizations could hire according to their beliefs even if it violated anti-discrimination laws.

Whether or not you agree with these executive orders is irrelevant. They created laws and are, therefore, not under the power of the president.

In his first presidential campaign, then candidate Barack Obama spoke out against these executive orders, campaigned heavily against them and promised to repeal them and close GITMO (Guantanamo Bay). He even signed an executive order to close GITMO within a year as his first act as president. He was expected to get rid of the above executive orders as well as some others. This is how it played out:

- Obama expanded the wiretap authority even more. One end of the line just had to be connected to a sponsor of terror, even if both parties were inside the US.

- Not via executive order, but through Congress, the ability to detain prisoners in GITMO was expanded. The National Defense Authorization Act (NDAA) is a law Congress uses to authorize the maintaining and funding of our military. However, for the first time in history, it now includes a clause that expands the detention at GITMO not only to include those caught on the battlefield, but also United States citizens. Suspected terrorists can be picked up in the United States and held based on the opinion of the executive branch. Furthermore, it is not required that they be given trials. In the event suspects are sent to trial and found innocent, they can continue to be held if the Obama administration still considers them a threat.

> President Obama did repeal the third one (faith-based organization can hire those who support of their beliefs.) The ironic thing is that this one should never have been an issue because this is not within the authority of the federal government. The original executive order by President GW Bush was unnecessary because it should have already been the case; therefore the second executive order by President BH Obama was also unconstitutional.

Here are some additional executive orders that have been signed by President Obama:
> 10990 – Allows the federal government to take control of all forms of transportation, all roads and all sea ports.

> 10995 – Allows the federal government to take control of the communication media including the Internet.

> 10997 – Allows the federal government to take control of power, gas, petroleum and minerals.

> 11000 – Allows the federal government to mobilize citizens into "worker brigades" (forced slavery).

> 11002 – Allows the postmaster general to create and operate a national registration of all people.

> 13603 – Allows for the federal government to declare martial law during times of peace.

There are those who deny this power exists here, but considering the long list of orders established that pertain to taking control of everything else, and President Obama's track record of abusing authority, I consider those who deny this power to be exercising hope over common sense.

The Founders of our country fled from a king because they did not believe in putting great power with any one man. The president is no exception.

An argument that defends the use of executive orders is the claim that every president all the way back to George Washington used them. Does that make it legal? No. Does that make it right? No. On what do they base this authority? Article II, Section 1, Clause 1:
  "*The executive Power shall be vested in a President of the United States of America.*"

Article II, Section 3, Clause 5:
  "*he shall take Care that the Laws be faithfully executed*"

I doubt that you see the power to create laws through executive order there any more than I do. So, let's look at executive orders from a historical perspective. Insuring that the laws be faithfully executed does not include creation of laws. It would, however, include following the limits on authority.

Prior to 1907, the term "executive order" was not used to describe an act by a president. This occurred when the government decided to document executive orders. They went back to Lincoln's Emancipation Proclamation and started numbering there with #1. Most, prior to Lincoln, were not actually written and were referred to at that time as "proclamations."

Arguments that George Washington used executive orders are laughable because Washington did not create law. His first, out of a total of two proclamations he made, was a request - not even a demand - that those who had been in the confederate government and were now in the new Constitutional government issue him a report.

In his second, he proclaimed:
> "Both Houses of Congress have by their joint Committee requested me to recommend to the People of the United States a day of public thanksgiving."

This pales in comparison to the expansive use of executive orders today. Consider that the first fifteen presidents issued an average of *less than ten* proclamations, and few if any attempted to create law in any way. Contrast that with today. Going all the way back to Kennedy, each president has issued an average of 150-190 executive orders per four-year term.

They use them to create laws, and they go around Congress to do so. We must not ignore that FDR was the king of executive orders issuing over 3500 of them.

There is one characteristic that all proclamations, executive orders, or any other names they have been called, possess. If executive orders created law, they were unconstitutional. Even Lincoln's *Emancipation Proclamation* held no legal standing. If it had, there would be no need for the 13th Amendment. The federal government knew that a proclamation by the president could not create law, so they passed the 13th, ensuring that abolishing slavery could not be ignored.

We have already discussed another major abuse by the executive branch which is the expansion of government through "agencies."

Since 1945, there have been 245 agencies created by the president issuing an executive order, by cabinet secretaries, or by executive reorganization. In other words, 245 agencies have been created without Congressional input or approval. The average budget for an agency created by the executive branch in today's dollars is $3.3 Billion. Granted, not all of those agencies are still around, but if only 200 of them are, that is $660 Billion every year for unconstitutional agencies.

Whether you think they are a good idea or not, they are clearly a violation of the Constitution. There are only two ways that such bodies should exist:

> If a constitutional amendment is passed to allow for such agencies.

> If state constitutions allow for such agencies, then it would be legal for states to create their own agencies.

Because this is not the case for any of the 240 agencies created by the executive branch, 100% of them are unconstitutional.

Legislative Abuses

By far, most abuses fall upon the shoulders of Congress, however many also involve one or both of the other branches of government to make them work. Unfortunately, what was designed as a system of checks and balances has become a system of collusion and favor trading and in the process is bypassing and completely eliminating the Constitution.

Let's go back to the agencies. Are agencies that were created by Congress constitutional? The answer is a resounding, maybe. Congress does have the authority to create agencies, <u>by law</u>. The power to appoint people to the judicial bench, appoint ambassadors, and appoint to agencies was given to the president so long as the agencies were created <u>by law</u>.

This means that Congress does have the authority to create agencies. However, Article I, Section 8 gives very finite limits on the powers of Congress and the Bill of Rights, and more specifically the 9th and 10th Amendments restate that all other powers are reserved to the states. This clearly shows that Congress can only create agencies for the purpose of carrying out the limited function of the federal government.

Are agencies that have been created by Congress constitutional? Most are not. The federal government was never intended to be large or powerful. It was intended to be a small body that takes care of only those issues that impact the nation as a whole. Agencies such as the DEA, FDA, EPA, Department of Energy, Department of Education, and about 1500 others are not within the powers of the federal government according to the Constitution. Any of those agencies which are not specifically necessary to carry out the limited role of the federal government are unconstitutional.

Aside from growth through agency creation, most abuses of authority that Congress perpetuates through legislation are justified by Congress using one of a few clauses.

Article I, Section 8, Paragraph 1 says:
"The Congress shall have Power To lay and collect Taxes, Duties, Imposts and Excises, to pay the Debts and provide for the common Defense and general Welfare of the United States; but all Duties, Imposts and Excises shall be uniform throughout the United States;"

The term "general welfare" is commonly misused as a statement that the federal government can do anything that is perceived as "for the good of the people."

There are several reasons why this is not only wrong, but ridiculous. First, the term *general* is used several times in the Constitution. In every case, it refers to the "general government" or "general principles." In other words, it is talking about the nation as a whole; the federal government as a whole or the Constitution as a whole. The term "general" is never used to describe anything individual. Neither the welfare of an individual or of a state is addressed by the term.

The whole of the Constitution makes it clear that the federal government is to deal with national issues and the state governments with state issues. The term "general welfare" was clearly used to describe the wellbeing of the nation.

Second, it is absurd to think that, within a document that puts forth very restrictive language limiting the scope and powers of the federal government, that they would have included a two word phrase to allow the federal government the power to expand to any level that they see fit. If that had been the intent of the founders, they could have summed up the powers of the federal government this way: "First you elect them, and then they rule you." No other wording would be needed because the government would, of course, not do anything that they did not feel was best for society, right?

The second abused phrase is in Article I, Section 8, Paragraph 18:

"To make all Laws which shall be necessary and proper for carrying into Execution the foregoing Powers, and all other Powers vested by this Constitution in the Government of the United States, or in any Department or Officer thereof."

Again, expansionists use a few words and pretend that doing so grants unlimited expansion of power. This time the phrase is, "necessary and proper."

Big government proponents claim that this allows for any law that the federal government considers, to be the necessary and proper role of government.

Not only does this not make sense for the same reasons that the term "general welfare" does not justify expansion, but when you look at the entire paragraph, it spells out that Congress can do what is necessary and proper for carrying out the powers granted to Congress in Article I, Section 8, as well as the powers granted to the rest of the federal government by the Constitution.

Next, we have the most abused clause in the Constitution. Article I, Section 8, Paragraph 3:
> "To regulate Commerce with foreign Nations, and among the several States, and with the Indian Tribes."

This clause has been used to justify rules and regulations on business and even private transactions. It has been beaten and abused to the point that it is a shock when the US Supreme Court strikes down an abuse by Congress. Even though judicial review is not their duty, if Congress goes so far that their lap dog SCOTUS says no, then they have gone to an unconstitutional level that boggles the mind. When Congress has used this clause to justify its actions, the SCOTUS has almost never struck down the law.

The misuse of these clauses and the idea that they can do anything they want have led the Congress to abuse their authority on so many fronts that it is staggering. Quite literally, many estimates put more than 90% of federal laws outside of the constitutional restrictions of their authority. I estimate that to be well above 99%.

When you consider that the entire role of the federal government could be boiled down to little more than national defense and international trade & relations, then add the fact that Congress was supposed to be a part-time post, meeting at least once per year, it is actually quite difficult to find a law that Congress has passed in the last 100 years in which they were strictly abiding by the Constitution.

Sooooo.....

How did we get here? There are a few things that have brought us to where we are today in this nation.

First, abuses by the federal government. They have abused the powers that have been given to them and they have literally seized power through intimidation, through false declaration, through bribery, and through indoctrination.

- **Intimidation:** When the federal government wants to pressure a state or all of the states to do something, they simply threaten to cut off funding for projects that, in many cases, they have mandated.

- **False Declaration:** This started when Chief Justice John Marshall declared that the federal government was bound not by the Constitution, but by their own discretion. This is the power that he stole that day for the federal government by declaring that the SCOTUS has the authority of judicial review. Since then, the legislative and executive branches have been able to get away with almost anything so long as they can get their partner, the SCOTUS, to sign off on it or, as is the case most often; people just believe that they have no recourse.

Many think that all of the laws that Congress passes and all executive orders that the president writes are reviewed by the SCOTUS. This is not the case at all. Very few are. They are only reviewed if they are challenged by states or by citizens. Proportionately, that almost never happens. When it does, it is even rarer that the SCOTUS sides with the states or the people over their partners in the federal government.

➢ **Bribery:** Much like intimidation but in reverse, the federal government will frequently offer favors for a state that will do what it says. It is also not uncommon for president to offer bribes, waivers, or other favors in exchange for support from a group or votes from a legislator. Legally, they cannot bribe a legislator by offering money for a vote, however it is no different to set aside discretionary budget money for a senator or representative's pet project in his state if they swing the vote the way the executive branch wants. These pet projects pander to voting blocks, or often to kickbacks directly or indirectly to the legislator. You didn't think that they end up increasing their net worth by millions of dollars on their salaries, did you?

➢ **Indoctrination:** This is exactly what it sounds like. Key phrases such as tolerance, fairness, and level the playing field are common throughout the education system of today. Yet, it is anything but fair, equal or tolerant.

Our kids are systematically taught. . .
- To blame the wealthy for the troubles in our country today.

- Poverty is caused by the greed of the wealthy.

- Keeping your money is greedy, but wanting the government to force others to give you their money is fair.

- Christians are intolerant and should be shunned.

- Nothing bad in your life is your fault. Society is to blame.

- The American dream is dead.

And most importantly - -
- You can trust the government. The government is your friend; the answer to all of society's problems.

- Most problems can be fixed by taking money from the wealthy.

Most recently, Common Core standards teach children to be angry; to have nothing but contempt and anger for parents and other authority figures. It is frightening.

Because kids would not otherwise go for such vile "education" if they question what is being taught, they must have ADHD. The answer is to drug them into a state of zombie obedience.

Some people might think I'm a bit dramatic here. I assure you; I have only scratched the surface. The anti-gun indoctrination has gotten so bad that kids are getting suspended or expelled for the shockingly horrifying acts of:

- Drawing a picture of a gun.

- Drawing a picture of a soldier with a gun.

- Pointing a chicken finger at a teacher.

- Playing cops and robbers at recess.

- Pointing the gun of a GI Joe action figure at another child.

These are a few examples of many. It is utter lunacy in public schools today, and it is only getting worse!

Furthermore, when you have elementary teachers teaching students to sing praises to the president - ANY president - that is wrong.

Then there is the problematic media. The media has become a lapdog for liberal politics and expansive government. Once upon a time, the media's high standards required that they report the news without bias. Over time, it has become more and more suspect of having a liberal bias. Around 1990, the media started to show a clear and undeniable bias in favor of liberal politics and democrats in general.

By the time of the candidacy of Barack Obama for president in 2008, the media jumped from bias clear over advocacy and into what can only be called a slobbering love affair. The blatant bias was not even hidden anymore. They detailed everything except Obama's lack of qualification, his associations, his anti-American writing in his books, and the few votes that he did make as an Illinois State and US Senator.

What did we hear about? His no-shirt beach vacation and how good he looked. That he was an amazing speaker…of course it was never mentioned that he sputtered and said more ums and ahs than words without his teleprompter. Then, of course there was the famous quote, the feeling that people get when they hear him speak. "I felt this thrill going up my leg. Now, I don't have that too often." – Chris Matthews
According to the media, Obama is a man who can do no wrong and they were more than happy to cover up anything negative about him.

Between the media, school, and Hollywood, it is no wonder that so many kids have no clue what is going on in the world of politics.

How Far Have We Gone?

Recently, through executive orders, President Obama has claimed the power to take over the following... and this is not a complete list.
- All forms of transportation
- All forms of communication
- The Internet
- All forms of money
- All forms of energy production.
- All forms of food production.

That is just a partial list. Obama has also signed executive orders to (unconstitutionally) grab the power to:
- Detain enemy combatants indefinitely, (remember he scolded President Bush for this, but he expanded it.) He can order them held even if found innocent.
- Order the assassination of US citizens outside of the US even if they are not involved in combat against the US.
- Order the assassination of US citizens inside of the US if they are involved in combative actions...and he defines the combative actions as he sees fit.
- Declare martial law even in times of peace.

Do not believe for a minute that these abuses started with Barack Obama. George W. Bush was not innocent of using executive orders for unconstitutional things. Neither was Clinton, George HW Bush, Reagan, etc. In reality, any executive order which actually creates law is unconstitutional and, by definition, null and void.

Next, let's take a look what is arguably the biggest financial abuse of power by the federal government. The Patient Protection and Affordable Care Act (PPACA), commonly referred to as Obamacare, has taken unconstitutional, as well as collusion by all three branches, to a new level.

During the discussions about PPACA, some members of Congress were asked about their authority to compel people to buy something that they do not want.

Nancy Pelosi was asked, "Madam Speaker, where specifically does the Constitution grant Congress the authority to enact an individual health insurance mandate?"

Her response was very enlightening. She replied, "Are you serious? Are you serious?" and moved on without even addressing the question.

Another example comes from Pete Stark; a US Congressman and one of the Constitutional scholars that "people for uncontrolled government" like to quote. In a town meeting, a woman asked Stark how the Affordable Care Act can be Constitutional when it forces one person to pay for another's product which, as she pointed out, is a form of slavery. A second part of her question asked Stark if the federal government can do this, what can they *not do* that impacts our private lives?

Congressman Stark answered, saying, "I think that there **are** very few Constitutional limits that would prevent the federal government from rules that could affect your private life. Now, the basis for that would be how does it affect other people?"

The young lady pressed about the limited powers enumerated by the Constitution leaving all other authority to the states or the people. She then repeated the two-part question about the Constitutionality of the Affordable Care Act and what the federal government could not do. She then followed with, "So is your answer that they can do anything?"

Congressman Stark responded, "The federal government can, yes, do most anything in this country."

It becomes very clear that legislators feel that they have absolutely no restrictions on what they can and cannot do.

The battle of the Constitutionality of PPACA raged on throughout the entire process until it was passed…sort of, (more on that in a minute). After it was signed into law, states immediately brought forth lawsuits against the federal government to block implementation of PPACA based on the fact that it is unconstitutional. This created its own problem as they were taking the fight to the Supreme Court which, as I have already shown, is not the final arbiter of the Constitutionality of a law. The states should have simply declared it unconstitutional. It did, however, get a hearing in front of the US Supreme Court. The decision was 5-4 that the law could stand, but not as argued.

Proponents of PPACA stressed throughout the entire process that it is not a tax, however there will be fines imposed on those who do not have proper health insurance. Congress claims that it has the right to do this under the Interstate Commerce clause because not purchasing insurance could cause prices to go up for everyone. This launched a whole host of spin and complete nonsense as to how not buying something can be regulated.

The Supreme Court disagreed, which is one of the few times that the Supreme Court has denied the use of the Interstate Commerce clause as a way of expanding the powers of the federal government. However, in yet another unprecedented action, the Supreme Court determined a way that the federal government could do this and fall within their interpretation of the Constitution. They ruled that this could be done under the taxing powers of the federal government.

This was unprecedented because the Supreme Court had never taken steps to rule against a party, but had instead given the party a way to change the ruling. In the past, such rulings would have simply been ruled unconstitutional under the interstate commerce clause. It is also the first time that citizens became eligible to be taxed for <u>not</u> buying a product.

Now, for the "sort of." Article I, Section 7, Paragraph 1 of the Constitution says:
"All Bills for raising Revenue shall originate in the House of Representatives; but the Senate may propose or concur with Amendments as on other Bills."

When the US Supreme Court ruled that this bill could only be Constitutional if it was a tax bill, that makes it a revenue bill. The version of the PPACA that was eventually signed by President Obama originated in the Senate. It was, therefore, never passed according to the laws of the US Constitution.

So we had the president pushing, and quite literally bribing members of Congress to pass the bill. One democrat representative, Eric Massa, even said that he was pushed around in the shower by Rham Emmanuel because he was going to vote no on the PPACA. He would not change, so they got rid of him.

Then, in a move that shocked the country, Chief Justice John Roberts (the deciding vote of the SCOTUS,) whom everyone knew was going to shoot it down, voted in favor of the PPACA. Many suggest that Roberts was either bought or threatened because at the last minute, he not only changed his vote, he devised the method where Obamacare would be legal in the opinion of the SCOTUS.

They declared that it could stand if the penalty was a tax and not a fee. This created two problems. First, as mentioned above, the "tax" title made it a revenue bill. Nobody has taken up that fight because Congress lacks the political will. The House may have voted to repeal more than 30 times, but if they truly wanted it gone, they would have declared that it never originated in the House, therefore is not law.

The second problem is that, no matter how the SCOTUS wants to do backflips to play nice with this president, their ruling was absurd. For anyone to say that the Constitution allows for a person to be taxed *for not buying a product* is ridiculous. The fact that the states have not simply said "NO!" is even more ridiculous.

So the president colluded with, bought, and threatened the Congress to pass this bill. We are unsure as to how they turned Chief Justice Roberts, but it was clearly a last minute change. So again, rather than a system of checks and balances, we now have a system of collusion.

Whether you support Obamacare or not, it is impossible to argue that it is Constitutional. It is also impossible to argue that it is the law of the land as it has never been passed. Finally, it is impossible to say that it is settled because the body that "settled" it has no such authority.

Other recent unconstitutional acts by the federal government and more specifically the Obama administration include:

- Giving guns to drug cartels in Mexico which led to the murder of several Mexican citizens and Americans as well.

- Giving money and weapons to groups who have declared hatred against America and Israel - first the Muslim Brotherhood and recently, Al Qaeda.

- Targeting and killing US Citizens by direction of the president without due process. This is conspiracy to commit murder, and then accessory to murder.

- Spying on US citizens' phone, Internet and other fronts. This one is breaking news as I type and is certain to get worse as we learn more.

- IRS using extreme scrutiny on TEA Party groups and those who affiliate with them for political reasons.

- No Child Left Behind (GW Bush) and Common Core (BH Obama). In no way does the federal government have the authority to be involved in our education system.

➢ Restrictions on what we can grow for our own consumption on our own land. This is under the guise of "protecting the food supply." Whether you believe that there are nefarious reasons for this, such as taking control of the food supply, or that it is "for our own good," this is clearly not within the limited power of the federal government.

➢ Unmanned drone surveillance. A clear violation of privacy rights.

➢ Last week, President Obama directed the EPA to set emission standards for corporations. This is a back-door enactment of Cap-n-Trade, which failed in Congress because the people do not want it. Add this to the fact that the EPA is not a constitutional agency; therefore Obama is using an unconstitutional agency to create laws, which is also a constitutional violation in a move to usurp the people and Congress.

I recently asked four US Senators, including the junior senator from my own state, Idaho, Senator Jim Risch, why Congress does not stop him. All four said that they did not know what they could do. Clearly, they think that the president is above them, not an equal branch of government. They did not even have the guts to try. They are defeated and weak.

Today, one of the big debates is gun laws. Once again, legislators are using false arguments to press their agendas. They pretend that creating gun laws will make us safer. This has been proven false time and time again. In his book, "More Guns, Less Crime," John Lott brings forth the most comprehensive study on the link between guns and gun violence that I have ever read. He blows the arguments for gun control out of the water. I highly recommend the book.

Rham Emmanuel once said, "Never let a serious crisis go to waste." The left lives by this philosophy. When there was a mass shooting at a Newtown, Connecticut elementary, they began crying for gun control. When there was a mass shooting at Virginia Tech, they called for tighter gun laws.

Proponents of gun control fail to acknowledge the obvious. All of these mass shootings, with the exception of the shooting in Arizona where former US Representative Gabrielle Giffords was shot, were in "gun-free zones." In other words, the law did not stop these killers. You do not see people shooting up NRA rallies and gun shows. There is a reason. Criminals like easy targets. Pickpockets avoid wallets on chains; burglars watch for signs that people are not home, and murderers avoid places where there are guns. It makes more sense to train and arm some teachers and/or staff.

Add the fact that within the past several years the vast majority of homicides in this country - and suicides for that matter, involve one common denominator: Mind altering drugs. These same drugs are banned in some European countries because, not only are they largely ineffective, but they are also clearly linked to an elevated number of suicides and homicides.

Over 75% of all ADD, ADHD and depression drugs prescribed to teens are prescribed in this country. It is no surprise that suicide and homicide rates for teens are also much higher in this country. It is time to stop poisoning our kids' minds and bodies with these horrible drugs. But that is a topic for another book.

Keep in mind that nothing that I have written here is an exhaustive list. They are samples of abuse of power, samples of betrayal, samples of what is truly a war against our children. If I tried to make an inclusive list, it would fill the Library of Congress. An inclusive list of government waste and fraud would be even longer. The US government is out of control and on a collision course with itself. It cannot possibly continue on the path that it is on. We must rein it in.

The federal government was designed to deal only with things that impact the country as a whole, but it has morphed into a huge, wasteful monstrosity that reaches into every area of our lives. It is out of control, it is bankrupting our nation. It is long past time to turn this country around and abide by the Constitution once again. It is time to put the power of the government back where the founders placed it - <u>with the states and the people</u>.

Chapter 4

United Again

The question that people ask me more than any other is, "Jon, haven't we gone too far to get back?"

No, we haven't. It will not be easy, but nothing worthwhile ever is. We must unite once again and demand more. Phrases like, "It is just politics," or, "You can't fight City Hall," must go away. When people use these phrases, urge them to get on board or at least stop shouting defeat and get out of the way.

How Do We Get It Back?

The first step in bringing this country back to the great nation that it once was is to establish where the true powers lie. So, if you are a believer, that power clearly rests with God. He has said that if we will humble ourselves and pray, he will hear us and heal our land. So, I will call this step, LARGE 1.

Pray. If you believe... *pray*. If you don't, what could it hurt?

For the rest, where do you believe that the highest power in this country lies? If you said, with the president, US Supreme Court, Congress, state legislatures, or the judges on American Idol, you are wrong. The highest power in the land rests with the **voters**.

Many will claim that voters do not matter because elections are rigged or because of voter fraud, etc. You are wrong. It is your responsibility to demand and insure that elections are fair. Demand such things from your state legislators as limiting early or absentee voting and voter ID laws. If they do not believe they can enact such laws, loan them your copy of this book. Stand up, gather forces and DEMAND that they act.

Remember - they work for you. You did not elect leaders; you elected servants to represent you. You have the right to tell them how you want to be represented. If they do not, you have the power to vote them out of office or recall them. After you remember that you are their boss - remind them. They have forgotten as well.

Some of you may be thinking that we're past the point of no return. If we keep doing what we have been doing and expect different results, you are right. We must take a bold approach. Desperate times call for desperate measures. What is that bold approach? We must fire all incumbents at their next election. Before you shrug this one off, it is necessary and it is easy, so read on.

How can we possibly fire them all? Do you know anyone who is not disgusted with the federal government? Democrats? Republicans? Green Party? Independents? Libertarians? Others? Of course you don't. People who are happy with the federal government are as rare as vegetarians at a hot dog eating contest.

This idea is so popular across the board that I have talked about it at TEA Party rallies and Occupy rallies, bringing the same message and getting standing ovations at both.

If all of us who are upset with those in Congress, then all we have to do is *show up*. Historically, non-presidential primaries have very low voter turnouts.

Looking at the last five election cycles, a 10% increase in registered voters showing up or newly voting for the challenger instead of the incumbent, would have turned the election in over 90% of all state and federal primary elections! A 5% increase would turn over 50% of them.

So many voters ignore the primary election because they think that only the general really matters. In reality, if you want a change in government, you must vote in the primary. If the same people keep electing the same incumbents in the primary, you have very little say in your general election, especially if you are in a dominantly republican or dominantly democrat district. In the primary, you are much more likely to help direct the outcome because voter turnout is much lower. If you want to toss out the incumbent, you are much more likely to accomplish this in the primary.

Also, in the primary, people do not have to vote against their party in order to get someone new. If people truly understood this, do you really think people like Barbara Boxer, Maxine Waters or John McCain would continue to get reelected? The same people show up at the primaries and vote for the same names that they have been voting for so long, that they have become lulled into a naive and dangerous comfort zone. If the voters in these districts would actually show up at the primaries, you may still see democrats in the seats of Boxer and Waters and a republican in McCain's seat...but it would likely not be those three.

If those of us who are tired of the government digging deeper into our daily lives and taking us farther from the Constitution, just show up. We can quite simply fire all incumbents.

"Jon, what about the good politicians? We don't want to throw the baby out with the bath water." This is an argument that I get more often than the claim that "it will never work" from those who have already forfeited.

Is there a politician out there at any level who has always voted with the Constitution, who has stood up for states' rights and has taken steps to stop the unconstitutional actions of Barack Obama, or presidents before him for that matter? If you truly do know of one that has done all of this and more, we need a presidential candidate a VP and governors, because we are firing them, too.

If you are one who believes that we only need to throw out the bad ones, turn to Appendix III right now. Read "Why Congress Never Changes," and then come back.

The next step is to tell the new Congress, state legislatures, governors, attorneys general and such exactly what we require and expect of them. It is not like we are making unjust demands. We are simply holding them accountable for performing and fulfilling

their oaths of office. The demands of state government are:
- Start nullifying all laws which are unconstitutional beginning with the stolen power of judicial review. It was never intended to rest with the courts, but with the states.
- Nullify PPACA. It is not law.
- Remove all infringements on the Bill of Rights.
- All states take back their own state lands. The federal government has no provision for controlling land outside of the seat of government.
- Enforce immigration laws. The Constitution granted the federal government the authority to determine what the laws should be, but enforcement of law is not within the mandate of the federal government.
- Take control of public education away from the federal government and put it back with local school boards and parents, where it belongs.

That should keep the state government busy for quite some time. They have a lot of laws to nullify. > Now let's move on to what we must demand from our federal government:
- Get rid of all federal regulations on business of any kind. The federal government has no authority to dictate how business should be done in this country unless it is to regulate interstate commerce. This is to ensure that one state cannot be harmed so another can benefit. Interstate

commerce, however, has nothing to do with controlling private business.
- Get rid of all unconstitutional federal agencies.
- Repeal the 17th Amendment. Force the Senate to do their job of <u>protecting states' rights</u>.
- Read and understand all legislation before voting on it.
- Declare all executive orders null and void as they are laws created by the executive branch.

Finally, you must share what you know. I am convinced that the person who originated the idea that one must never talk politics or religion in a civilized society was an Atheist politician who wanted people to be ignorant of both faith and politics. If you are a person of faith, it is selfish not to share with others how to get to heaven. As for politics, keeping silent is what has brought us so far away from the Constitution.

Politics needs to be the topic of conversation until such time as people start taking action. Complacency has brought us here, and we will continue down the wrong road if we continue to be complacent. Don't ram it down people's throats, but encourage them to get educated and participate. Show people your passion for this country and be sincere about the positive impact that can be made.

Wrapping It All Up

The federal government has very little Constitutional authority. They have been stealing more and more power since day one, and along the way they have gradually convinced us that they are in control. It is time to put the federal government back in its proper position. This is a project that is very simple, but it will not be easy. Here are the simple steps each of us can take:

- Get involved. Contact your legislators and remind them that they are not your leaders, but your selected servants and tell them exactly what you expect of them.
- Get more involved. Join your Republican or Democratic National Convention precinct committees. Be involved in the discussions that impact you.
- Vote! In the *primary* as well as the general.
- Pay attention. Look at the voting records of the new batch of legislators over the next term. Know if they are following their oath of office or betraying it. If you don't know where to look, ask someone that you truly trust to tell you without imposing their agenda, or ask more than one person.
- Share what you have learned with others around you. Don't sit back and let a few power hungry politicians overstep their authority and destroy our rights.

- Consider running for political office. We will be needing candidates who are committed to upholding their oath to support and defend the Constitution.
- Learn your rights and stand up for them. If you will not defend your rights, you have none.

There it is. It is that simple. The changes will not happen overnight and the process will not be easy, but nothing worthwhile ever is.

A Final Thought

There is a belief that the government granted us the rights spelled out in the Bill of Rights. That is not the case. The Bill of Rights did not "grant" us those rights, it acknowledged them. Whether you call these natural rights or, to use a term from the Declaration of Independence, rights endowed by our Creator, they are rights that we have and the Bill of Rights simply identifies and acknowledges those rights. The government has no authority whatsoever to impede or infringe upon those rights in any way.

Stand up for your rights. If you will not stand up for them, you will lose them.

Appendix 1

*-As I stated in the beginning pages of this book, any direct copying of the Constitution or any other founding document is strictly with original spelling and punctuation. In this appendix, underlined sections are those changed or eliminated by the amendments.

The Constitution of the United States of America

We the People of the United States, in Order to form a more perfect Union, establish Justice, insure domestic Tranquility, provide for the common defence, promote the general Welfare, and secure the Blessings of Liberty to ourselves and our Posterity, do ordain and establish this Constitution for the United States of America.

Article. I.

Section. 1.

All legislative Powers herein granted shall be vested in a Congress of the United States, which shall consist of a Senate and House of Representatives.

Section. 2.

The House of Representatives shall be composed of Members chosen every second Year by the People of the several States, and the Electors in each State shall have the Qualifications requisite for Electors of the most numerous Branch of the State Legislature.

No Person shall be a Representative who shall not have attained to the Age of twenty five Years, and been seven Years a Citizen of the United States, and who shall not, when elected, be an Inhabitant of that State in which he shall be chosen.

<u>Representatives and direct Taxes shall be apportioned among the several States which may be included within this Union, according to their respective Numbers, which shall be determined by adding to the whole Number of free Persons, including those bound to Service for a Term of Years, and excluding Indians not taxed, three fifths of all other Persons</u>. The actual Enumeration shall be made within three Years after the first Meeting of the Congress of the United States, and within every subsequent Term of ten Years, in such Manner as they shall by Law direct. The Number of Representatives shall not exceed one for every thirty Thousand, but each State shall have at Least one Representative; and until such enumeration shall be made, the State of New Hampshire shall be entitled to chuse three, Massachusetts eight, Rhode-Island and Providence Plantations one, Connecticut five, New-York six, New Jersey four, Pennsylvania eight, Delaware one, Maryland six, Virginia ten, North Carolina five, South Carolina five, and Georgia three.

When vacancies happen in the Representation from any State, the Executive Authority thereof shall issue Writs of Election to fill such Vacancies.

The House of Representatives shall chuse their Speaker and other Officers; and shall have the sole Power of Impeachment.

Section. 3.

The Senate of the United States shall be composed of two Senators from each State, <u>chosen by the</u>

Legislature thereof for six Years; and each Senator shall have one Vote.

Immediately after they shall be assembled in Consequence of the first Election, they shall be divided as equally as may be into three Classes. The Seats of the Senators of the first Class shall be vacated at the Expiration of the second Year, of the second Class at the Expiration of the fourth Year, and of the third Class at the Expiration of the sixth Year, so that one third may be chosen every second Year; and if Vacancies happen by Resignation, or otherwise, during the Recess of the Legislature of any State, the Executive thereof may make temporary Appointments until the next Meeting of the Legislature, which shall then fill such Vacancies.

No Person shall be a Senator who shall not have attained to the Age of thirty Years, and been nine Years a Citizen of the United States, and who shall not, when elected, be an Inhabitant of that State for which he shall be chosen.

The Vice President of the United States shall be President of the Senate, but shall have no Vote, unless they be equally divided.

The Senate shall chuse their other Officers, and also a President pro tempore, in the Absence of the Vice President, or when he shall exercise the Office of President of the United States.

The Senate shall have the sole Power to try all Impeachments. When sitting for that Purpose, they shall be on Oath or Affirmation. When the President of the United States is tried, the Chief Justice shall preside: And no Person shall be convicted without the Concurrence of two thirds of the Members present.

Judgment in Cases of Impeachment shall not extend further than to removal from Office, and disqualification to hold and enjoy any Office of honor, Trust or Profit under the United States: but the Party convicted shall nevertheless be liable and subject to Indictment, Trial, Judgment and Punishment, according to Law.

Section. 4.

The Times, Places and Manner of holding Elections for Senators and Representatives, shall be prescribed in each State by the Legislature thereof; but the Congress may at any time by Law make or alter such Regulations, except as to the Places of chusing Senators.

The Congress shall assemble at least once in every Year, and such Meeting shall <u>be on the first Monday in December</u>, unless they shall by Law appoint a different Day.

Section. 5.

Each House shall be the Judge of the Elections, Returns and Qualifications of its own Members, and a Majority of each shall constitute a Quorum to do Business; but a smaller Number may adjourn from day to day, and may be authorized to compel the Attendance of absent Members, in such Manner, and under such Penalties as each House may provide.

Each House may determine the Rules of its Proceedings, punish its Members for disorderly Behaviour, and, with the Concurrence of two thirds, expel a Member.

Each House shall keep a Journal of its Proceedings, and from time to time publish the same, excepting such Parts as may in their Judgment require Secrecy; and the Yeas and Nays of the Members of either House on any question shall, at the Desire of one fifth of those Present, be entered on the Journal.

Neither House, during the Session of Congress, shall, without the Consent of the other, adjourn for more than three days, nor to any other Place than that in which the two Houses shall be sitting.

Section. 6.

The Senators and Representatives shall receive a Compensation for their Services, to be ascertained by Law, and paid out of the Treasury of the United States. They shall in all Cases, except Treason, Felony and Breach of the Peace, be privileged from Arrest during their Attendance at the Session of their respective Houses, and in going to and returning from the same; and for any Speech or Debate in either House, they shall not be questioned in any other Place.

No Senator or Representative shall, during the Time for which he was elected, be appointed to any civil Office under the Authority of the United States, which shall have been created, or the Emoluments whereof shall have been encreased during such time; and no Person holding any Office under the United States, shall be a Member of either House during his Continuance in Office.

Section. 7.

All Bills for raising Revenue shall originate in the House of Representatives; but the Senate may propose or concur with Amendments as on other Bills.

Every Bill which shall have passed the House of Representatives and the Senate, shall, before it become a Law, be presented to the President of the United States: If he approve he shall sign it, but if not he shall return it, with his Objections to that House in which it shall have originated, who shall enter the Objections at large on their Journal, and proceed to reconsider it. If after such Reconsideration two thirds of that House shall agree to pass the Bill, it shall be sent, together with the Objections, to the other House, by which it shall likewise be reconsidered, and if approved by two thirds of that House, it shall become a Law. But in all such Cases the Votes of both Houses shall be determined by yeas and Nays, and the Names of the Persons voting for and against the Bill shall be entered on the Journal of each House respectively. If any Bill shall not be returned by the President within ten Days (Sundays excepted) after it shall have been presented to him, the same shall be a Law, in like Manner as if he had signed it, unless the Congress by their Adjournment prevent its Return, in which Case it shall not be a Law.

Every Order, Resolution, or Vote to which the Concurrence of the Senate and House of Representatives may be necessary (except on a question of Adjournment) shall be presented to the President of the United States; and before the Same shall take Effect, shall be approved by him, or being disapproved by him, shall be repassed by two thirds of the Senate and House of Representatives, according to the Rules and Limitations prescribed in the Case of a Bill.

Section. 8.

The Congress shall have Power To lay and collect Taxes, Duties, Imposts and Excises, to pay the Debts and provide for the common Defence and general Welfare of the United States; but all Duties, Imposts and Excises shall be uniform throughout the United States;

To borrow Money on the credit of the United States;

To regulate Commerce with foreign Nations, and among the several States, and with the Indian Tribes;

To establish an uniform Rule of Naturalization, and uniform Laws on the subject of Bankruptcies throughout the United States;

To coin Money, regulate the Value thereof, and of foreign Coin, and fix the Standard of Weights and Measures;

To provide for the Punishment of counterfeiting the Securities and current Coin of the United States;

To establish Post Offices and post Roads;

To promote the Progress of Science and useful Arts, by securing for limited Times to Authors and Inventors the exclusive Right to their respective Writings and Discoveries;

To constitute Tribunals inferior to the Supreme Court;

To define and punish Piracies and Felonies committed on the high Seas, and Offences against the Law of Nations;

To declare War, grant Letters of Marque and Reprisal, and make Rules concerning Captures on Land and Water;

To raise and support Armies, but no Appropriation of Money to that Use shall be for a longer Term than two Years;

To provide and maintain a Navy;

To make Rules for the Government and Regulation of the land and naval Forces;

To provide for calling forth the Militia to execute the Laws of the Union, suppress Insurrections and repel Invasions;

To provide for organizing, arming, and disciplining, the Militia, and for governing such Part of them as may be employed in the Service of the United States, reserving to the States respectively, the Appointment of the Officers, and the Authority of training the Militia according to the discipline prescribed by Congress;

I Want My Country Back

To exercise exclusive Legislation in all Cases whatsoever, over such District (not exceeding ten Miles square) as may, by Cession of particular States, and the Acceptance of Congress, become the Seat of the Government of the United States, and to exercise like Authority over all Places purchased by the Consent of the Legislature of the State in which the Same shall be, for the Erection of Forts, Magazines, Arsenals, dock-Yards, and other needful Buildings; And to make all Laws which shall be necessary and proper for carrying into Execution the foregoing Powers, and all other Powers vested by this Constitution in the Government of the United States, or in any Department or Officer thereof.

Section. 9.

The Migration or Importation of such Persons as any of the States now existing shall think proper to admit, shall not be prohibited by the Congress prior to the Year one thousand eight hundred and eight, but a Tax or duty may be imposed on such Importation, not exceeding ten dollars for each Person.

The Privilege of the Writ of Habeas Corpus shall not be suspended, unless when in Cases of Rebellion or Invasion the public Safety may require it.

No Bill of Attainder or ex post facto Law shall be passed.

No Capitation, or other direct, Tax shall be laid, <u>unless in Proportion to the Census or enumeration herein before directed to be taken</u>.

No Tax or Duty shall be laid on Articles exported from any State.

No Preference shall be given by any Regulation of Commerce or Revenue to the Ports of one State over those of another; nor shall Vessels bound to, or from, one State, be obliged to enter, clear, or pay Duties in another.

No Money shall be drawn from the Treasury, but in Consequence of Appropriations made by Law; and a regular Statement and Account of the Receipts and Expenditures of all public Money shall be published from time to time.

No Title of Nobility shall be granted by the United States: And no Person holding any Office of Profit or Trust under them, shall, without the Consent of the Congress, accept of any present, Emolument, Office, or Title, of any kind whatever, from any King, Prince, or foreign State.

Section. 10.

No State shall enter into any Treaty, Alliance, or Confederation; grant Letters of Marque and Reprisal; coin Money; emit Bills of Credit; make any Thing but gold and silver Coin a Tender in Payment of Debts; pass any Bill of Attainder, ex post facto Law, or Law impairing the Obligation of Contracts, or grant any Title of Nobility.

No State shall, without the Consent of the Congress, lay any Imposts or Duties on Imports or Exports, except what may be absolutely necessary for executing it's inspection Laws: and the net Produce of all Duties and Imposts, laid by any State on Imports or Exports, shall be for the Use of the Treasury of the United States; and all such Laws shall be subject to the Revision and Controul of the Congress.

No State shall, without the Consent of Congress, lay any Duty of Tonnage, keep Troops, or Ships of War in time of Peace, enter into any Agreement or Compact with another State, or with a foreign Power, or engage in War, unless actually invaded, or in such imminent Danger as will not admit of delay.

Article. II.

Section. 1.

The executive Power shall be vested in a President of the United States of America. He shall hold his Office during the Term of four Years, and, together with the Vice President, chosen for the same Term, be elected, as follows:

Each State shall appoint, in such Manner as the Legislature thereof may direct, a Number of Electors, equal to the whole Number of Senators and Representatives to which the State may be entitled in the Congress: but no Senator or Representative, or Person holding an Office of Trust or Profit under the United States, shall be appointed an Elector.

<u>The Electors shall meet in their respective States, and vote by Ballot for two Persons, of whom one at least shall not be an Inhabitant of the same State with</u>

themselves. And they shall make a List of all the Persons voted for, and of the Number of Votes for each; which List they shall sign and certify, and transmit sealed to the Seat of the Government of the United States, directed to the President of the Senate. The President of the Senate shall, in the Presence of the Senate and House of Representatives, open all the Certificates, and the Votes shall then be counted. The Person having the greatest Number of Votes shall be the President, if such Number be a Majority of the whole Number of Electors appointed; and if there be more than one who have such Majority, and have an equal Number of Votes, then the House of Representatives shall immediately chuse by Ballot one of them for President; and if no Person have a Majority, then from the five highest on the List the said House shall in like Manner chuse the President. But in chusing the President, the Votes shall be taken by States, the Representation from each State having one Vote; A quorum for this purpose shall consist of a Member or Members from two thirds of the States, and a Majority of all the States shall be necessary to a Choice. In every Case, after the Choice of the President, the Person having the greatest Number of Votes of the Electors shall be the Vice President. But if there should remain two or more who have equal Votes, the Senate shall chuse from them by Ballot the Vice President.

The Congress may determine the Time of chusing the Electors, and the Day on which they shall give their Votes; which Day shall be the same throughout the United States.

No Person except a natural born Citizen, or a Citizen of the United States, at the time of the Adoption of this Constitution, shall be eligible to the Office of President; neither shall any Person be eligible to that Office who shall not have attained to the Age of thirty five Years, and been fourteen Years a Resident within the United States.

<u>In Case of the Removal of the President from Office, or of his Death, Resignation, or Inability to discharge the Powers and Duties of the said Office, the Same shall devolve on the Vice President, and the Congress may by Law provide for the Case of Removal, Death, Resignation or Inability, both of the President and Vice President, declaring what Officer shall then act as President, and such Officer shall act accordingly, until the Disability be removed, or a President shall be elected</u>.

The President shall, at stated Times, receive for his Services, a Compensation, which shall neither be increased nor diminished during the Period for which he shall have been elected, and he shall not receive within that Period any other Emolument from the United States, or any of them.

Before he enter on the Execution of his Office, he shall take the following Oath or Affirmation:--"I do solemnly swear (or affirm) that I will faithfully execute the Office of President of the United States, and will to the best of my Ability, preserve, protect and defend the Constitution of the United States."

Section. 2.

The President shall be Commander in Chief of the Army and Navy of the United States, and of the Militia of the several States, when called into the actual Service of the United States; he may require the Opinion, in writing, of the principal Officer in each of the executive Departments, upon any Subject relating to the Duties of their respective Offices, and he shall have Power to grant Reprieves and Pardons for Offences against the United States, except in Cases of Impeachment.

He shall have Power, by and with the Advice and Consent of the Senate, to make Treaties, provided two thirds of the Senators present concur; and he shall nominate, and by and with the Advice and Consent of the Senate, shall appoint Ambassadors, other public Ministers and Consuls, Judges of the supreme Court, and all other Officers of the United States, whose Appointments are not herein otherwise provided for, and which shall be established by Law: but the Congress may by Law vest the Appointment of such inferior Officers, as they think proper, in the President alone, in the Courts of Law, or in the Heads of Departments.

The President shall have Power to fill up all Vacancies that may happen during the Recess of the Senate, by granting Commissions which shall expire at the End of their next Session.

Section. 3.

He shall from time to time give to the Congress Information of the State of the Union, and recommend to their Consideration such Measures as he shall judge necessary and expedient; he may, on extraordinary Occasions, convene both Houses, or either of them, and in Case of Disagreement between them, with Respect to the Time of Adjournment, he may adjourn them to such Time as he shall think proper; he shall receive Ambassadors and other public Ministers; he shall take Care that the Laws be faithfully executed, and shall Commission all the Officers of the United States.

Section. 4.

The President, Vice President and all civil Officers of the United States, shall be removed from Office on Impeachment for, and Conviction of, Treason, Bribery, or other high Crimes and Misdemeanors.

Article III.

Section. 1.

The judicial Power of the United States shall be vested in one Supreme Court and in such inferior Courts as the Congress may from time to time ordain and establish. The Judges, both of the supreme and inferior Courts, shall hold their Offices during good Behaviour, and shall, at stated Times, receive for their Services a Compensation, which shall not be diminished during their Continuance in Office.

Section. 2.

The judicial Power shall extend to all Cases, in Law and Equity, arising under this Constitution, the Laws of the United States, and Treaties made, or which shall be made, under their Authority;--to all Cases affecting Ambassadors, other public Ministers and Consuls;--to all Cases of admiralty and maritime Jurisdiction;--to Controversies to which the United States shall be a Party;--to Controversies between two or more States;-- <u>between a State and Citizens of another State</u>,--between Citizens of different States,--between Citizens of the same State claiming Lands under Grants of different States, and between a State, or the Citizens thereof, and foreign States, Citizens or Subjects.

In all Cases affecting Ambassadors, other public Ministers and Consuls, and those in which a State shall be Party, the Supreme Court shall have original Jurisdiction. In all the other Cases before mentioned, the Supreme Court shall have appellate Jurisdiction, both as to Law and Fact, with such Exceptions, and under such Regulations as the Congress shall make.

The Trial of all Crimes, except in Cases of Impeachment, shall be by Jury; and such Trial shall be held in the State where the said Crimes shall have been committed; but when not committed within any State, the Trial shall be at such Place or Places as the Congress may by Law have directed.

Section. 3.

Treason against the United States shall consist only in levying War against them, or in adhering to their

Enemies, giving them Aid and Comfort. No Person shall be convicted of Treason unless on the Testimony of two Witnesses to the same overt Act, or on Confession in open Court.

The Congress shall have Power to declare the Punishment of Treason, but no Attainder of Treason shall work Corruption of Blood, or Forfeiture except during the Life of the Person attainted.

Article. IV.

Section. 1.

Full Faith and Credit shall be given in each State to the public Acts, Records, and judicial Proceedings of every other State. And the Congress may by general Laws prescribe the Manner in which such Acts, Records and Proceedings shall be proved, and the Effect thereof.

Section. 2.

The Citizens of each State shall be entitled to all Privileges and Immunities of Citizens in the several States.

A Person charged in any State with Treason, Felony, or other Crime, who shall flee from Justice, and be found in another State, shall on Demand of the executive Authority of the State from which he fled, be delivered up, to be removed to the State having Jurisdiction of the Crime.

<u>No Person held to Service or Labour in one State, under the Laws thereof, escaping into another, shall, in</u>

<u>Consequence of any Law or Regulation therein, be discharged from such Service or Labour, but shall be delivered up on Claim of the Party to whom such Service or Labour may be due</u>.

Section. 3.

New States may be admitted by the Congress into this Union; but no new State shall be formed or erected within the Jurisdiction of any other State; nor any State be formed by the Junction of two or more States, or Parts of States, without the Consent of the Legislatures of the States concerned as well as of the Congress.

The Congress shall have Power to dispose of and make all needful Rules and Regulations respecting the Territory or other Property belonging to the United States; and nothing in this Constitution shall be so construed as to Prejudice any Claims of the United States, or of any particular State.

Section. 4.

The United States shall guarantee to every State in this Union a Republican Form of Government, and shall protect each of them against Invasion; and on Application of the Legislature, or of the Executive (when the Legislature cannot be convened), against domestic Violence.

Article. V.

The Congress, whenever two thirds of both Houses shall deem it necessary, shall propose Amendments to this Constitution, or, on the Application of the Legislatures of two thirds of the several States, shall call a Convention for proposing Amendments, which, in either Case, shall be valid to all Intents and Purposes, as Part of this Constitution, when ratified by the Legislatures of three fourths of the several States, or by Conventions in three fourths thereof, as the one or the other Mode of Ratification may be proposed by the Congress; Provided that no Amendment which may be made prior to the Year One thousand eight hundred and eight shall in any Manner affect the first and fourth Clauses in the Ninth Section of the first Article; and that no State, without its Consent, shall be deprived of its equal Suffrage in the Senate.

Article. VI.

All Debts contracted and Engagements entered into, before the Adoption of this Constitution, shall be as valid against the United States under this Constitution, as under the Confederation.

This Constitution, and the Laws of the United States which shall be made in Pursuance thereof; and all Treaties made, or which shall be made, under the Authority of the United States, shall be the supreme Law of the Land; and the Judges in every State shall be bound thereby, any Thing in the Constitution or Laws of any State to the Contrary notwithstanding.

The Senators and Representatives before mentioned, and the Members of the several State Legislatures, and all executive and judicial Officers, both of the United States and of the several States, shall be bound by Oath or Affirmation, to support this Constitution; but no religious Test shall ever be required as a Qualification to any Office or public Trust under the United States.

Article. VII.

The Ratification of the Conventions of nine States shall be sufficient for the Establishment of this Constitution between the States so ratifying the same.

The Word, "the," being interlined between the seventh and eighth Lines of the first Page, the Word "Thirty" being partly written on an Erazure in the fifteenth Line of the first Page, The Words "is tried" being interlined between the thirty second and thirty third Lines of the first Page and the Word "the" being interlined between the forty third and forty fourth Lines of the second Page.

Attest William Jackson Secretary

done in Convention by the Unanimous Consent of the States present the Seventeenth Day of September in the Year of our Lord one thousand seven hundred and Eighty seven and of the Independance of the United States of America the Twelfth In witness whereof We have hereunto subscribed our Names,

The Bill of Rights: A Transcription

The Preamble to The Bill of Rights

Congress of the United States begun and held at the City of New-York, on Wednesday the fourth of March, one thousand seven hundred and eighty nine.

THE Conventions of a number of the States, having at the time of their adopting the Constitution, expressed a desire, in order to prevent misconstruction or abuse of its powers, that further declaratory and restrictive clauses should be added: And as extending the ground of public confidence in the Government, will best ensure the beneficent ends of its institution.

RESOLVED by the Senate and House of Representatives of the United States of America, in Congress assembled, two thirds of both Houses concurring, that the following Articles be proposed to the Legislatures of the several States, as amendments to the Constitution of the United States, all, or any of which Articles, when ratified by three fourths of the said Legislatures, to be valid to all intents and purposes, as part of the said Constitution; viz.

ARTICLES in addition to, and Amendment of the Constitution of the United States of America, proposed by Congress, and ratified by the Legislatures of the several States, pursuant to the fifth Article of the original Constitution.

Note: The following text is a transcription of the first ten amendments to the Constitution in their original form. These amendments were ratified December 15, 1791, and form what is known as the "Bill of Rights."

Amendment I

Congress shall make no law respecting an establishment of religion, or prohibiting the free exercise thereof; or abridging the freedom of speech, or of the press; or the right of the people peaceably to assemble, and to petition the Government for a redress of grievances.

Amendment II

A well regulated Militia, being necessary to the security of a Free State, the right of the people to keep and bear Arms, shall not be infringed.

Amendment III

No Soldier shall, in time of peace be quartered in any house, without the consent of the Owner, nor in time of war, but in a manner to be prescribed by law.

Amendment IV

The right of the people to be secure in their persons, houses, papers, and effects, against unreasonable searches and seizures, shall not be violated, and no Warrants shall issue, but upon probable cause, supported by Oath or affirmation, and particularly describing the place to be searched, and the persons or things to be seized.

Amendment V

No person shall be held to answer for a capital, or otherwise infamous crime, unless on a presentment or indictment of a Grand Jury, except in cases arising in the land or naval forces, or in the Militia, when in actual service in time of War or public danger; nor shall any person be subject for the same offence to be twice put in jeopardy of life or limb; nor shall be compelled in any criminal case to be a witness against himself, nor be deprived of life, liberty, or property, without due process of law; nor shall private property be taken for public use, without just compensation.

Amendment VI

In all criminal prosecutions, the accused shall enjoy the right to a speedy and public trial, by an impartial jury of the State and district wherein the crime shall have been committed, which district shall have been previously ascertained by law, and to be informed of the nature and cause of the accusation; to be confronted with the witnesses against him; to have compulsory process for obtaining witnesses in his favor, and to have the Assistance of Counsel for his defence.

Amendment VII

In Suits at common law, where the value in controversy shall exceed twenty dollars, the right of trial by jury shall be preserved, and no fact tried by a jury, shall be otherwise re-examined in any Court of the United States, than according to the rules of the common law.

Amendment VIII

Excessive bail shall not be required, nor excessive fines imposed, nor cruel and unusual punishments inflicted.

Amendment IX

The enumeration in the Constitution, of certain rights, shall not be construed to deny or disparage others retained by the people.

Amendment X

The powers not delegated to the United States by the Constitution, nor prohibited by it to the States, are reserved to the States respectively, or to the people.

Amendments 11-27

AMENDMENT XI
Passed by Congress March 4, 1794. Ratified February 7, 1795.

Note: Article III, section 2, of the Constitution was modified by amendment 11.

The Judicial power of the United States shall not be construed to extend to any suit in law or equity, commenced or prosecuted against one of the United States by Citizens of another State, or by Citizens or Subjects of any Foreign State.

AMENDMENT XII
Passed by Congress December 9, 1803. Ratified June 15, 1804.

Note: A portion of Article II, section 1 of the Constitution was superseded by the 12th amendment.

The Electors shall meet in their respective states and vote by ballot for President and Vice-President, one of whom, at least, shall not be an inhabitant of the same state with themselves; they shall name in their ballots the person voted for as President, and in distinct ballots the person voted for as Vice-President, and they shall make distinct lists of all persons voted for as President, and of all persons voted for as Vice-President, and of the number of votes for each, which lists they shall sign and certify, and transmit sealed to the seat of the government of the United States, directed to the President of the Senate; -- the President of the Senate shall, in the presence of the Senate and House of Representatives, open all the certificates and the votes shall then be counted; -- The person having the greatest number of votes for President, shall be the President, if such number be a majority of the whole number of Electors appointed; and if no person have such majority, then from the persons having the highest numbers not exceeding three on the list of those voted for as President, the House of Representatives shall choose immediately, by ballot, the President. But in choosing the President, the votes shall be taken by states, the representation from each state having one vote; a quorum for this purpose shall consist of a member or members from two-thirds of the states, and a majority of all the states shall be necessary to a choice. [And if the House of Representatives shall not choose a President whenever the right of choice shall devolve upon them, before the fourth day of March next following, then the Vice-President shall act as President, as in case of the death or other constitutional disability of the President. --]* The person having the greatest number of votes as Vice-President, shall be the Vice-President, if such number be a majority of the whole number of Electors appointed, and if no person have a majority, then from the two highest numbers on the list, the Senate shall choose the Vice-President; a quorum for the purpose shall consist of two-thirds of the whole number of Senators, and a majority of the whole number shall be necessary to a choice. But no person constitutionally ineligible to the office of President shall be eligible to that of Vice-President of the United States.

*Superseded by section 3 of the 20th amendment.

AMENDMENT XIII

Passed by Congress January 31, 1865. Ratified December 6, 1865.

Note: A portion of Article IV, section 2, of the Constitution was superseded by the 13th amendment.

Section 1. Neither slavery nor involuntary servitude, except as a punishment for crime whereof the party shall have been duly convicted, shall exist within the United States, or any place subject to their jurisdiction.

Section 2. Congress shall have power to enforce this article by appropriate legislation.

AMENDMENT XIV

Passed by Congress June 13, 1866. Ratified July 9, 1868.

Note: Article I, section 2, of the Constitution was modified by section 2 of the 14th amendment.

Section 1. All persons born or naturalized in the United States, and subject to the jurisdiction thereof, are citizens of the United States and of the State wherein they reside. No State shall make or enforce any law which shall abridge the privileges or immunities of citizens of the United States; nor shall any State deprive any person of life, liberty, or property, without due process of law; nor deny to any person within its jurisdiction the equal protection of the laws.

Section 2. Representatives shall be apportioned among the several States according to their respective numbers, counting the whole number of persons in each State, excluding Indians not taxed. But when the right to vote at any election for the choice of electors for President and Vice-President of the United States, Representatives in Congress, the Executive and Judicial officers of a State, or the members of the Legislature thereof, is denied to any of the male inhabitants of such State, being twenty-one years of age,* and citizens of the United States, or in any way abridged, except for participation in rebellion, or other crime, the basis of representation therein shall be reduced in the proportion which the number of such male citizens shall bear to the whole number of male citizens twenty-one years of age in such State.

Section 3. No person shall be a Senator or Representative in Congress, or elector of President and Vice-President, or hold any office, civil or military, under the States, or under any State, who, having previously taken an oath, as a member of Congress, or as an officer of the United States, or as a member of any State legislature, or as an executive or judicial officer of any State, to support the Constitution of the United States, shall have engaged in insurrection or rebellion against the same, or given aid or comfort to the enemies thereof. But Congress may by a vote of two-thirds of each House, remove such disability.

Section 4. The validity of the public debt of the United States, authorized by law, including debts incurred for payment of pensions and bounties for services in suppressing insurrection or rebellion, shall not be questioned. But neither the United States nor any State shall assume or pay any debt or obligation incurred in aid of insurrection or rebellion against the United States, or any claim for the loss or emancipation of any slave; but all such debts, obligations and claims shall be held illegal and void.

Section 5. The Congress shall have the power to enforce, by appropriate legislation, the provisions of this article.

*Changed by section 1 of the 26th amendment.

AMENDMENT XV

Passed by Congress February 26, 1869. Ratified February 3, 1870.

Section 1. The right of citizens of the United States to vote shall not be denied or abridged by the United States or by any State on account of race, color, or previous condition of servitude--

Section 2. The Congress shall have the power to enforce this article by appropriate legislation.

AMENDMENT XVI

Passed by Congress July 2, 1909. Ratified February 3, 1913.

Note: Article I, section 9, of the Constitution was modified by amendment 16.

The Congress shall have power to lay and collect taxes on incomes, from whatever source derived, without apportionment among the several States, and without regard to any census or enumeration.

AMENDMENT XVII
Passed by Congress May 13, 1912. Ratified April 8, 1913.

Note: Article I, section 3, of the Constitution was modified by the 17th amendment.

The Senate of the United States shall be composed of two Senators from each State, elected by the people thereof, for six years; and each Senator shall have one vote. The electors in each State shall have the qualifications requisite for electors of the most numerous branch of the State legislatures.

When vacancies happen in the representation of any State in the Senate, the executive authority of such State shall issue writs of election to fill such vacancies: *Provided*, That the legislature of any State may empower the executive thereof to make temporary appointments until the people fill the vacancies by election as the legislature may direct.

This amendment shall not be so construed as to affect the election or term of any Senator chosen before it becomes valid as part of the Constitution.

AMENDMENT XVIII

Passed by Congress December 18, 1917. Ratified January 16, 1919. Repealed by amendment 21.

Section 1. After one year from the ratification of this article the manufacture, sale, or transportation of intoxicating liquors within, the importation thereof into, or the exportation thereof from the United States and all territory subject to the jurisdiction thereof for beverage purposes is hereby prohibited.

Section 2. The Congress and the several States shall have concurrent power to enforce this article by appropriate legislation.

Section 3. This article shall be inoperative unless it shall have been ratified as an amendment to the Constitution by the legislatures of the several States, as provided in the Constitution, within seven years from the date of the submission hereof to the States by the Congress.

AMENDMENT XIX

Passed by Congress June 4, 1919. Ratified August 18, 1920.

The right of citizens of the United States to vote shall not be denied or abridged by the United States or by any State on account of sex.

Congress shall have power to enforce this article by appropriate legislation.

AMENDMENT XX

Passed by Congress March 2, 1932. Ratified January 23, 1933.

Note: Article I, section 4, of the Constitution was modified by section 2 of this amendment. In addition, a portion of the 12th amendment was superseded by section 3.

Section 1. The terms of the President and the Vice President shall end at noon on the 20th day of January, and the terms of Senators and Representatives at noon on the 3rd day of January, of the years in which such terms would have ended if this article had not been ratified; and the terms of their successors shall then begin.

Section 2. The Congress shall assemble at least once in every year, and such meeting shall begin at noon on the 3d day of January, unless they shall by law appoint a different day.

Section 3. If, at the time fixed for the beginning of the term of the President, the President elect shall have died, the Vice President elect shall become President. If a President shall not have been chosen before the time fixed for the beginning of his term, or if the President elect shall have failed to qualify, then the Vice President elect shall act as President until a President shall have qualified; and the Congress may by law provide for the case wherein neither a President elect nor a Vice President shall have qualified, declaring who shall then act as President, or the manner in which one who is to act shall be selected, and such person shall act accordingly until a President or Vice President shall have qualified.

Section 4. The Congress may by law provide for the case of the death of any of the persons from whom the House of Representatives may choose a President whenever the right of choice shall have devolved upon them, and for the case of the death of any of the persons from whom the Senate may choose a Vice President whenever the right of choice shall have devolved upon them.

Section 5. Sections 1 and 2 shall take effect on the 15th day of October following the ratification of this article.

Section 6. This article shall be inoperative unless it shall have been ratified as an amendment to the Constitution by the legislatures of three-fourths of the several States within seven years from the date of its submission.

AMENDMENT XXI
Passed by Congress February 20, 1933. Ratified December 5, 1933.

Section 1. The eighteenth article of amendment to the Constitution of the United States is hereby repealed.

Section 2. The transportation or importation into any State, Territory, or Possession of the United States for delivery or use therein of intoxicating liquors, in violation of the laws thereof, is hereby prohibited.

Section 3. This article shall be inoperative unless it shall have been ratified as an amendment to the Constitution by conventions in the several States, as provided in the Constitution, within seven years from the date of the submission hereof to the States by the Congress.

AMENDMENT XXII

Passed by Congress March 21, 1947. Ratified February 27, 1951.

Section 1. No person shall be elected to the office of the President more than twice, and no person who has held the office of President, or acted as President, for more than two years of a term to which some other person was elected President shall be elected to the office of President more than once. But this Article shall not apply to any person holding the office of President when this Article was proposed by Congress, and shall not prevent any person who may be holding the office of President, or acting as President, during the term within which this Article becomes operative from holding the office of President or acting as President during the remainder of such term.

Section 2. This article shall be inoperative unless it shall have been ratified as an amendment to the Constitution by the legislatures of three-fourths of the several States within seven years from the date of its submission to the States by the Congress.

AMENDMENT XXIII

Passed by Congress June 16, 1960. Ratified March 29, 1961.

Section 1. The District constituting the seat of Government of the United States shall appoint in such manner as Congress may direct:

A number of electors of President and Vice President equal to the whole number of Senators and Representatives in Congress to which the District would be entitled if it were a State, but in no event more than the least populous State; they shall be in addition to those appointed by the States, but they shall be considered, for the purposes of the election of President and Vice President, to be electors appointed by a State; and they shall meet in the District and perform such duties as provided by the twelfth article of amendment.

Section 2. The Congress shall have power to enforce this article by appropriate legislation.

AMENDMENT XXIV
Passed by Congress August 27, 1962. Ratified January 23, 1964.

Section 1. The right of citizens of the United States to vote in any primary or other election for President or Vice President, for electors for President or Vice President, or for Senator or Representative in Congress, shall not be denied or abridged by the United States or any State by reason of failure to pay poll tax or other tax.

Section 2. The Congress shall have power to enforce this article by appropriate legislation.

AMENDMENT XXV

Passed by Congress July 6, 1965. Ratified February 10, 1967.

Note: Article II, section 1, of the Constitution was affected by the 25th amendment.

Section 1. In case of the removal of the President from office or of his death or resignation, the Vice President shall become President.

Section 2. Whenever there is a vacancy in the office of the Vice President, the President shall nominate a Vice President who shall take office upon confirmation by a majority vote of both Houses of Congress.

Section 3. Whenever the President transmits to the President pro tempore of the Senate and the Speaker of the House of Representatives his written declaration that he is unable to discharge the powers and duties of his office, and until he transmits to them a written declaration to the contrary, such powers and duties shall be discharged by the Vice President as Acting President.

Section 4. Whenever the Vice President and a majority of either the principal officers of the executive departments or of such other body as Congress may by law provide, transmit to the President pro tempore of the Senate and the Speaker of the House of Representatives their written declaration that the President is unable to discharge the powers and duties of his office, the Vice President shall immediately assume the powers and duties of the office as Acting President.

Thereafter, when the President transmits to the President pro tempore of the Senate and the Speaker of the House of Representatives his written declaration that no inability exists, he shall resume the powers and duties of his office unless the Vice President and a majority of either the principal officers of the executive department or of such other body as Congress may by law provide, transmit within four days to the President pro tempore of the Senate and the Speaker of the House of Representatives their written declaration that the President is unable to discharge the powers and duties of his office. Thereupon Congress shall decide the issue, assembling within forty-eight hours for that purpose if not in session. If the Congress, within twenty-one days after receipt of the latter written declaration, or, if Congress is not in session, within twenty-one days after Congress is required to assemble, determines by two-thirds vote of both Houses that the President is unable to discharge the powers and duties of his office, the Vice President shall continue to discharge the same as Acting President; otherwise, the President shall resume the powers and duties of his office.

AMENDMENT XXVI
Passed by Congress March 23, 1971. Ratified July 1, 1971.

Note: Amendment 14, section 2, of the Constitution was modified by section 1 of the 26th amendment.

Section 1. The right of citizens of the United States, who are eighteen years of age or older, to vote shall not be denied or abridged by the United States or by any State on account of age.

Section 2. The Congress shall have power to enforce this article by appropriate legislation.

AMENDMENT XXVII
Originally proposed <u>Sept. 25, 1789</u>. Ratified May 7, 1992.

No law, varying the compensation for the services of the Senators and Representatives, shall take effect, until an election of representatives shall have intervened.

Appendix 2
The Kentucky Resolutions of 1798

1. *Resolved*, That the several States composing, the United States of America, are not united on the principle of unlimited submission to their general government; but that, by a compact under the style and title of a Constitution for the United States, and of amendments thereto, they constituted a general government for special purposes — delegated to that government certain definite powers, reserving, each State to itself, the residuary mass of right to their own self-government; and that whensoever the general government assumes undelegated powers, its acts are unauthoritative, void, and of no force: that to this compact each State acceded as a State, and is an integral part, its co-States forming, as to itself, the other party: that the government created by this compact was not made the exclusive or final judge of the extent of the powers delegated to itself; since that would have made

its discretion, and not the Constitution, the measure of its powers; but that, as in all other cases of compact among powers having no common judge, each party has an equal right to judge for itself, as well of infractions as of the mode and measure of redress.

2. *Resolved*, That the Constitution of the United States, having delegated to Congress a power to punish treason, counterfeiting the securities and current coin of the United States, piracies, and felonies committed on the high seas, and offenses against the law of nations, and no other crimes, whatsoever; and it being true as a general principle, and one of the amendments to the Constitution having also declared, that "the powers not delegated to the United States by the Constitution, not prohibited by it to the States, are reserved to the States respectively, or to the people," therefore the act of Congress, passed on the 14th day of July, 1798, and intituled "An Act in addition to the act intituled An Act for the punishment of certain crimes against the United States," as also the act passed by them on the — day of June, 1798, intituled "An Act to punish frauds committed on the bank of the United States," (and all their other acts which assume to create, define, or punish crimes, other than those so enumerated in the Constitution,) are altogether void, and of no force; and that the power to create, define, and punish such other crimes is reserved, and, of right, appertains solely and exclusively to the respective States, each within its own territory.

3. *Resolved*, That it is true as a general principle, and is also expressly declared by one of the amendments to

the Constitutions, that "the powers not delegated to the United States by the Constitution, our prohibited by it to the States, are reserved to the States respectively, or to the people"; and that no power over the freedom of religion, freedom of speech, or freedom of the press being delegated to the United States by the Constitution, nor prohibited by it to the States, all lawful powers respecting the same did of right remain, and were reserved to the States or the people: that thus was manifested their determination to retain to themselves the right of judging how far the licentiousness of speech and of the press may be abridged without lessening their useful freedom, and how far those abuses which cannot be separated from their use should be tolerated, rather than the use be destroyed. And thus also they guarded against all abridgment by the United States of the freedom of religious opinions and exercises, and retained to themselves the right of protecting the same, as this State, by a law passed on the general demand of its citizens, had already protected them from all human restraint or interference. And that in addition to this general principle and express declaration, another and more special provision has been made by one of the amendments to the Constitution, which expressly declares, that "Congress shall make no law respecting an establishment of religion, or prohibiting the free exercise thereof, or abridging the freedom of speech or of the press": thereby guarding in the same sentence, and under the same words, the freedom of religion, of speech, and of the press: insomuch, that whatever violated either, throws down the sanctuary which covers the others, arid that libels, falsehood, and defamation, equally with heresy and false religion, are withheld from the cognizance of federal tribunals. That, therefore, the act of Congress of the United States, passed on the 14th day of July, 1798, intituled "An Act in addition to the act intituled An Act for the punishment of certain crimes against the United States," which does abridge the freedom of the press, is not law, but is altogether void, and of no force.

4. *Resolved*, That alien friends are under the jurisdiction and protection of the laws of the State wherein they are: that no power over them has been delegated to the United States, nor prohibited to the individual States, distinct from their power over citizens. And it being true as a general principle, and one of the amendments to the Constitution having also declared, that "the powers not delegated to the United States by the Constitution, nor prohibited by it to the States, are reserved to the States respectively, or to the people," the act of the Congress of the United States, passed on the — day of July, 1798, intituled "An Act concerning aliens," which assumes powers over alien friends, not delegated by the Constitution, is not law, but is altogether void, and of no force.

5. *Resolved*. That in addition to the general principle, as well as the express declaration, that powers not delegated are reserved, another and more special provision, inserted in the Constitution from abundant caution, has declared that "the migration or importation of such persons as any of the States now

existing shall think proper to admit, shall not be prohibited by the Congress prior to the year 1808" that this commonwealth does admit the migration of alien friends, described as the subject of the said act concerning aliens: that a provision against prohibiting their migration, is a provision against all acts equivalent thereto, or it would be nugatory: that to remove them when migrated, is equivalent to a prohibition of their migration, and is, therefore, contrary to the said provision of the Constitution, and void.

6. *Resolved*, That the imprisonment of a person under the protection of the laws of this commonwealth, on his failure to obey the simple order of the President to depart out of the United States, as is undertaken by said act intituled "An Act concerning aliens" is contrary to the Constitution, one amendment to which has provided that "no person shalt be deprived of liberty without due progress of law"; and that another having provided that "in all criminal prosecutions the accused shall enjoy the right to public trial by an impartial jury, to be informed of the nature and cause of the accusation, to be confronted with the witnesses against him, to have compulsory process for obtaining witnesses in his favor, and to have the assistance of counsel for his defense;" the same act, undertaking to authorize the President to remove a person out of the United States, who is under the protection of the law, on his own suspicion, without accusation, without jury, without public trial, without confrontation of the witnesses against him, without heating witnesses in his favor, without defense, without counsel, is contrary to

the provision also of the Constitution, is therefore not law, but utterly void, and of no force: that transferring the power of judging any person, who is under the protection of the laws from the courts, to the President of the United States, as is undertaken by the same act concerning aliens, is against the article of the Constitution which provides that "the judicial power of the United States shall be vested in courts, the judges of which shall hold their offices during good behavior"; and that the said act is void for that reason also. And it is further to be noted, that this transfer of judiciary power is to that magistrate of the general government who already possesses all the Executive, and a negative on all Legislative powers.

7. *Resolved*, That the construction applied by the General Government (as is evidenced by sundry of their proceedings) to those parts of the Constitution of the United States which delegate to Congress a power "to lay and collect taxes, duties, imports, and excises, to pay the debts, and provide for the common defense and general welfare of the United States," and "to make all laws which shall be necessary and proper for carrying into execution, the powers vested by the Constitution in the government of the United States, or in any department or officer thereof," goes to the destruction of all limits prescribed to their powers by the Constitution: that words meant by the instrument to be subsidiary only to the execution of limited powers, ought not to be so construed as themselves to give unlimited powers, nor a part to be so taken as to destroy the whole residue of that instrument: that the

proceedings of the General Government under color of these articles, will be a fit and necessary subject of revisal and correction, at a time of greater tranquility, while those specified in the preceding resolutions call for immediate redress.

8th. *Resolved*, That a committee of conference and correspondence be appointed, who shall have in charge to communicate the preceding resolutions to the Legislatures of the several States: to assure them that this commonwealth continues in the same esteem of their friendship and union which it has manifested from that moment at which a common danger first suggested a common union: that it considers union, for specified national purposes, and particularly to those specified in their late federal compact, to be friendly, to the peace, happiness and prosperity of all the States: that faithful to that compact, according to the plain intent and meaning in which it was understood and acceded to by the several parties, it is sincerely anxious for its preservation: that it does also believe, that to take from the States all the powers of self-government and transfer them to a general and consolidated government, without regard to the special delegations and reservations solemnly agreed to in that compact, is not for the peace, happiness or prosperity of these States; and that therefore this commonwealth is determined, as it doubts not its co-States are, to submit to undelegated, and consequently unlimited powers in no man, or body of men on earth: that in cases of an abuse of the delegated powers, the members of the general government, being chosen by the people, a change by the people would be the constitutional remedy; but, where powers are assumed which have not been delegated, a nullification of the act is the rightful remedy: that every State has a natural right in cases not within the compact, (*casus non fœderis*) to nullify of their own authority all assumptions of power by others within their limits: that without this right, they would be under the dominion, absolute and unlimited, of whosoever might exercise this right of judgment for them: that nevertheless, this commonwealth, from motives of regard and respect for its co States, has wished to communicate with them on the subject: that with them alone it is proper to communicate, they alone being parties to the compact, and solely authorized to judge in the last resort of the powers exercised under it, Congress being not a party, but merely the creature of the compact, and subject as to its assumptions of power to the final judgment of those by whom, and for whose use itself and its powers were all created and modified: that if the acts before specified should stand, these conclusions would flow from them; that the general government may place any act they think proper on the list of crimes and punish it themselves whether enumerated or not enumerated by the constitution as cognizable by them: that they may transfer its cognizance to the President, or any other person, who may himself be the accuser, counsel, judge and jury, whose suspicions may be the evidence, his order the sentence, his officer the executioner, and his breast the sole record of the transaction: that a very numerous and valuable description of the inhabitants of these States being, by this precedent, reduced, as outlaws, to the absolute dominion of one man, and the barrier of the Constitution thus swept away from us all, no ramparts now remains against the passions and the powers of a majority in Congress to protect from a like exportation, or other more grievous punishment, the minority of the same body, the legislatures, judges, governors and counsellors of the States, nor their other peaceable inhabitants, who may venture to reclaim the constitutional rights and liberties of the States and people, or who for other causes, good or bad, may be obnoxious to the views, or marked by the suspicions of the President, or be thought dangerous to his or their election, or other interests, public or personal; that the friendless alien has indeed been selected as the safest subject of a first experiment; but the citizen will soon follow, or rather, has already followed, for already has a sedition act marked him as its prey: that these and successive acts of the same character, unless arrested at the threshold, necessarily drive these States into revolution and blood and will furnish new calumnies against republican government, and new pretexts for those who wish it to be believed that man cannot be governed but by a rod of iron: that it would be a dangerous delusion were a confidence in the men of our choice to silence our fears for the safety of our rights: that confidence is everywhere the parent of despotism — free government is founded in jealousy, and not in confidence; it is jealousy and not confidence which prescribes limited constitutions, to bind down those whom we are obliged to trust with power: that our Constitution has accordingly fixed the limits to which, and no further, our confidence may go; and let the honest advocate of confidence read the Alien and Sedition acts, and say if the Constitution has not been wise in fixing limits to the government it created, and whether we should be wise in destroying those limits, Let him say what the government is, if it be not a tyranny, which the men of our choice have con erred on our President, and the President of our choice has assented to, and accepted over the friendly stranger to whom the mild spirit of our country and its law have pledged hospitality and protection: that the men of our choice have more respected the bare suspicion of the President, than the solid right of innocence, the claims of justification, the sacred force of truth, and the forms and substance of law and justice. In questions of powers, then, let no more be heard of confidence in man, but bind him down from mischief by the chains of the Constitution. That this commonwealth does therefore call on its co-States for an expression of their sentiments on the acts concerning aliens and for the punishment of certain crimes herein before specified, plainly declaring whether these acts are or are not authorized by the federal compact. And it doubts not that their sense will be so announced as to prove their attachment unaltered to limited government, weather general or particular. And that the rights and liberties of their co-States will be exposed to no dangers by remaining embarked in a common bottom with their own. That they will concur with this commonwealth in considering the said acts as so palpably against the

Constitution as to amount to an undisguised declaration that that compact is not meant to be the measure of the powers of the General Government, but that it will proceed in the exercise over these States, of all powers whatsoever: that they will view this as seizing the rights of the States, and consolidating them in the hands of the General Government, with a power assumed to bind the States (not merely as the cases made federal, casus fœderis but), in all cases whatsoever, by laws made, not with their consent, but by others against their consent: that this would be to surrender the form of government we have chosen, and live under one deriving its powers from its own will, and not from our authority; and that the co-States, recurring to their natural right in cases not made federal, will concur in declaring these acts void, and of no force, and will each take measures of its own for providing that neither these acts, nor any others of the General Government not plainly and intentionally authorized by the Constitution, shalt be exercised within their respective territories.

9th. *Resolved*, That the said committee be authorized to communicate by writing or personal conference, at any times or places whatever, with any person or persons who may be appointed by any one or more co-States to correspond or confer with them; and that they lay their proceedings before the next session of Assembly.

Appendix 3
Why Congress Never Changes

If you are not aware, a term for a large group of baboons is a "congress." It is not the most widely used or accepted, but perhaps it should be. The similarities between the actions of monkeys and politicians are strikingly similar.

Consider an experiment that was performed on a group of monkeys in a large cage. In the cage was a large rock mountain. Every day scientists conducting the experiment would lower a bunch of bananas onto the top of the mountain. The monkeys would begin climbing the rocks to get to the bananas, but when they were halfway there, the scientists would spray the monkeys with water. After a few days some of the monkeys stopped trying. However, all the monkeys were still sprayed if even one tried to get to the bananas. Pretty soon, if any monkeys started to climb, the others would pull them down and beat them in an effort to keep them from getting to the halfway point, which meant they would all get sprayed.

When all the monkeys stopped trying to get to the bananas, scientists replaced 20% of the monkeys with new monkeys. When the new monkeys tried to get to the bananas, the original monkeys would pull them down and beat them before they got to the halfway point.

When the new batch of monkeys stopped trying, they replaced another 20%, then another, until all of the monkeys had been replaced. After 5 cycles there was not one monkey that had ever been hosed down, yet any monkey that tried to get to the bananas was pulled down and beaten by the others.

This analogy shows exactly why replacing members of Congress a few at a time does not lead to better results, and why a full firing of all incumbents in every race in the 2014 primary elections has become so vital. If only a few members of Congress are replaced at a time, older members will overpower and impose their beliefs on new members. The cycle repeats itself endlessly, so regardless of the strength and conviction of new members, older members will overpower and nothing changes.

I Want My Country Back

About the Author

Who am I? I am a Christian, a family man, a serial entrepreneur, an author, a professional speaker, and a coach.

Over the years, I have built and sold several businesses, coached hundreds of business people and public speakers, and trained over 100,000 others…I have written a sales book titled, *"If Your Product Sells Itself, Shut UP!"*

I am also a patriot who believes in the American Dream. I am however saddened by the great divide in this country. That is why I wrote this book. I believe that we must unite to preserve and revitalize the American Dream.

I welcome and encourage feedback, stories, input and even disagreement. Please send any correspondence to UnitedAgain@YourVN.net

www.ingramcontent.com/pod-product-compliance
Lightning Source LLC
Chambersburg PA
CBHW051803040426
42446CB00007B/487